I0142016

Travis Tooke is the perfect person to write this book. He approaches all aspects of his life with the same ferocity he has with jiu-jitsu: he's committed to learning about it from the best sources and becoming an expert by putting in thousands of hours. You're sure to be informed and inspired.

—Andrew Craig, UFC fighter

I've known Travis for most of my time in the sport of mixed martial arts. He is honestly one of the best Brazilian Jiu-Jitsu black belts I've ever rolled with and has always been an inspiration. His dedication shows in his continued improvement as a Brazilian Jiu-Jitsu black belt competitor and instructor. This is evident in his students' performance in competition as well. Through commitment and dedication, this book shows us how the joy of something you're passionate about can lead to doors being opened that we never imagined accessible to us.

—Yves Edwards, UFC fighter and former #1 Lightweight

Jiu-Jitsu and Life

Lessons Learned on and off the Mat

TRAVIS TOOKE

Copyright 2020 Travis Tooke

All rights reserved. Except as permitted under the
US Copyright Act of 1976, no part of this publication
may be reproduced, distributed, or transmitted in any
form or by any means, or stored in a database or
retrieval system,without the prior written permission
of the publisher.

Writers of the Round Table Press
PO Box 1603, Deerfield, IL 60015
www.roundtablecompanies.com

Editor: **James Cook**
Cover Designer: **Sunny DiMartino**
Interior Designer: **Christy Bui**
Proofreaders: **Adam Lawrence, Carly Cohen**

Printed in the United States of America

First Edition: July 2020
10 9 8 7 6 5 4 3 2 1

Library of Congress Cataloging-in-Publication Data
Tooke, Travis.
Jiu-jitsu and life: lessons learned on and off the mat / Travis Tooke.—1st ed. p. cm.
ISBN Paperback: 978-1-61066-084-6
ISBN Digital: 978-1-61066-085-3
Library of Congress Control Number: 2020906536

Writers of the Round Table Press and the logo
are trademarks of Writers of the Round Table, Inc.

To my fellow martial artists, dreamers, entrepreneurs,
and risk-takers.

Your largest fear carries your greatest growth.
—Unknown

Contents

Introduction

In 2019, I celebrated fourteen years of owning a martial arts academy and thirty-eight years of being alive. That meant I'd spent over one-third of my life as a coach, a mentor, and a friend to martial arts students and peers (and nearly two-thirds of my life as a student). It also meant I'd spent one-third of my life working through challenges, trials, and failures in order to turn my passion for jiu-jitsu into a viable career.

Fourteen years is a big deal, since most martial arts schools close down within three to five years of opening. It's an accomplishment I don't take lightly—nor is it something that simply grew naturally out of the aptitude for jiu-jitsu I discovered as a teenager. It was far from easy.

But overcoming the odds to thrive in such a challenging business is not what I'm most proud of. The thing that puts a smile on my face day after day is also the very thing that can temporarily paralyze me. I'm talking about fear. Every day, fear pops up and tries to scare me away from doing something I really want to do or going after my goals. Does it ever win? Yes. I am not immune to fear. Some days it can get the better of me, and I'll delay or bail on doing something that would take me closer to a goal I really want to achieve—whether that's to grow my business or my jiu-jitsu practice.

But do I face the fear again the next day? Absolutely. The truth is that we need fear; it's how our species survived. Being truly fearless would likely earn you an early death. Alligator wrestlers, grizzly bear bow hunters, illegal bungee jumpers—they shouldn't feel totally relaxed and optimistic. These things can kill you!

In this book, I'll be telling my story. It's not just a martial arts story, a business story, or a story of my life, but it's a little bit of all three. Ultimately, it's a story about mindset, goals, passion, risk-taking, and, most importantly, it's about never giving up no matter the circumstances. I screwed up . . . a lot (it's a good thing I'm not a grizzly bear bow hunter). But I also did a lot of things right. I hope my journey helps you, whether you're pursuing a black belt, starting a business, or following a dream.

If you're a kid living in a mobile home with only the vaguest idea of what your future holds, or a complete newbie at business scared about making enough to pay the bills, or someone who has had some success but doesn't know the next step—I feel you. I've been there.

Ultimately, I want this book to inspire you to pursue the life you want in spite of the fear. The number one regret of dying people is, "I wish I'd had the courage to live a life true to myself, not the life others expected of me."[1] I want you to find the courage to find your true calling and pursue it regardless of what others—family members, well-wishers, and haters—may say.

I hope my story inspires you to chase your dreams no matter what they are: opening a school, becoming a UFC champion, starting a business, becoming a nuclear physicist, or whatever matters to you. As you pursue them, though, fear will trick you into asking, "What if I lose?" I've asked this question a lot. But facing that fear will invite you to ask a new question: "What if I win?"

1   Bronnie Ware, *The Top Five Regrets of the Dying: A Life Transformed by the Dearly Departing* (Carlsbad, CA: Hay House, 2011), 227.

*When we deny ourselves the ability to feel pain for
a purpose, we deny ourselves the ability to feel any
purpose in our life at all.*

—Mark Manson[2]

Skills are cheap. Passion is priceless.

—Gary Vaynerchuk[3]

CHAPTER 1

Passion and Purpose

Finding My Passion

It had been about three years since my parents divorced. I was fourteen,
living in a mobile home park with my mom on the outskirts of Houston,
when a friend rented some early UFC tapes (also known at the time as
"human cockfighting") from the local video store. I knew nothing about
it, but my interest was piqued.

"You mean like tae kwon do?" I asked, when Eric invited me over to
check them out.

"No," he replied. "These are real fights—no rules."

We plopped down on the couch in his living room, cued up the VCR,
and within minutes, I was leaning forward, shouting, "Wow, look at
that guy," and "did you see that?! Run it back!" as I watched real martial
artists applying their craft. We couldn't believe the world we'd stumbled upon. I'd taken my share of karate classes when I was in elementary
school, but this was *nothing* like those classes. This was exciting. These
grown men were tearing each other apart inside a chain-link cage—pick-
ing opponents up as if they were life-sized dolls, then slamming them

---

2   Mark Manson, *Everything Is F*cked: A Book About Hope* (New York: HarperCollins, 2019), 191

3   Gary Vaynerchuk, *Crush It!: Why NOW Is the Time to Cash In on Your Passion* (New York: HarperCollins, 2009), 9.

down on the mat or pinning them up against the fence.

Then this skinny little guy named Royce Gracie came out and started beating everybody with his jiu-jitsu moves. At six feet and a mere 176 pounds, he completely dominated everyone he fought and made it look easy. One of his signature moves was the rear naked choke, a technique that cuts off the blood supply from your opponent, forcing them to either tap out or blackout. He was also one of the only fighters wearing a gi (the traditional uniform used for martial arts), so his opponents couldn't escape from him as easily as they could from others whose skin was slick with sweat.

Royce Gracie's fighting was one of the coolest things I'd ever seen. I knew nothing of jiu-jitsu's mental components, nor could I have guessed at that early stage that jiu-jitsu would become a lifelong passion and career. All I knew was that Gracie had blown my mind. He made it look so fun that I wanted to start learning everything I could about this fascinating sport immediately.

I was hooked. From then on at home I wouldn't shut up about jiu-jitsu. I kept trying to force my younger brother to wrestle with me (he wasn't always up for it, believe it or not).

Then one day my mom was working out at a local gym when she spotted a flyer advertising jiu-jitsu classes at the martial arts academy next door. In support of my new obsession—and/or to save her own sanity—she signed me up. About a week later I was front and center at Champion Martial Arts, standing on a training mat in my first stiff, dull-white gi.

The class began with a mandatory four-hour orientation to introduce us to the fundamentals and sparring. I was so amped up about this opportunity that I had no concept of going "light." I was fifteen years old in a class full of adults, and I was determined to prove myself. I took it so seriously that when it came time to bow out (the bow martial artists typically take at the end of a match), I felt like I was going to throw up. I was so exhausted I went home and passed out in bed by six p.m. I didn't wake up until ten a.m. the next day.

After that, I returned to the school a couple of times a week to take jiu-jitsu classes. I also practiced the other martial arts the school taught—that was required to qualify for moving up the ranks in belt training—but my heart was always into jiu-jitsu. The sport was so new that none of the teachers really knew how to teach us much about it, so they just showed us whatever small grappling moves they could. The instructor had taken a few classes from some members of the Gracie family as well as Carlos Machado but had limited training in the art. It was good enough to get me started in the right direction. Any amount of formal instruction was better than what my friends and I had been doing up to that point, which basically involved slamming each other around on pieces of insulation foam we'd pieced together like a giant puzzle in the backyard. To this day I'm surprised that somebody didn't get really hurt during those ridiculous "matches."

But the more I learned, the more I wanted to know. So in addition to practicing at home every day after school, I entered local tournaments. In similar academies around town, we were all doing our best to figure out all the moves we could. No classes in the area focused solely on jiu-jitsu, but a handful of schools offered some form of grappling, whether it was judo, sambo, or modified "gringo" jiu-jitsu. Even then I sensed the struggle of trying to grow without continually seeking out peers who challenge you. We just had to be a little more resourceful when it came to finding jiu-jitsu-specific opportunities. In most cases, even when it came to tournaments, we were just a handful of people with some exposure to jiu-jitsu (mostly through VHS tapes, since the internet was still in its infancy) and a little background in traditional martial arts training, standing in dingy, fluorescent-lit rooms in our sweaty gis, ready to take each other on. No one had even developed a scoring system yet to determine winners. It was mostly left up to the coaches to decide. But the more we competed against each other, the better we got and the more quickly we learned new techniques. During class I got thrown around, wrestled to the ground, and tapped out more times than I can count, but I also earned some wins against adults who were much bigger than me.

• • •

Despite all of that initial enthusiasm and success, when I was sixteen, I decided to take a break from martial arts. It wasn't like anything happened, per se; it was more that I'd decided the stuff I did at fifteen was no longer "cool."

But after a couple of months, I got a call from Siggy, a woman I'd trained with at Champion. Surprised to hear her distinctive German accent, I wondered how and why she'd tracked me down.

"The last time I saw you was when you won that tournament at Alvis's studio a few months back," she said. "You really did great winning in overtime! It was not an easy win. We were all impressed, especially Alvis."

"Oh, thanks!" I said. "That's so cool to hear."

I was starting to feel glad she'd called. Alvis Solis, who owned a martial arts school across town from me, was one of the only blue belts in Houston at that time. (The blue belt is the second rung in the five-degree ladder that culminates in a black belt.) I'd seen him train once before at a seminar, but other than that, I didn't know him well.

"Still training hard?" she asked.

"Not really," I replied. "I kind of decided to take a break."

"Oh, really?" she said. She sounded surprised, and I felt myself flush. "Why's that? You were always so into it at Champions."

"No reason, really, just school and stuff . . ." I didn't say anything else. Looking back, I think maybe I was just being a teenager.

"I get it," she said. "School can be time-consuming, for sure. Anyway, Alvis is looking to build a pure jiu-jitsu program, and your name came up. I told him I'd find out if anyone at Champion knew how to get in touch with you. If you want, he says you can come train for free for the rest of the summer."

That short call reminded me how much I still enjoyed jiu-jitsu. And I'd be training for free? Free is hard to pass up, especially when free is about all you can afford. By the time I hung up the phone, I was already excited.

So at age sixteen, in my busted-ass car with no AC, I made the ninety-minute roundtrip drive across steaming-hot Houston five or six times a week, getting in as much practice and training as I possibly could. Once I was back, it was like I'd never stopped training at all. It felt like coming home. Sometimes I'd even go twice a day. What I lacked in technical proficiency I made up for with just the grind of going to Alvis's school every day, trying again and again.

One of the handful of students in the class was this guy Doug, a tough-as-hell country boy who constantly kicked my ass. He wasn't a huge guy. In fact, his frame was about the same as mine, only his had more meat on it. We'd spar a lot, and he would always kick my butt. For the life of me, I just could not beat him—until one day, after several minutes of surviving another beating, I finally caught him in an arm bar.

I didn't celebrate externally, of course—that would be bad form—but in my head it was like fireworks were going off. *Oh my God! I did it!*

That's exactly how it happens in jiu-jitsu. Just like a lot of things in life, you don't have a lot of giant breakthroughs. You have a few little victories amid a lot of getting beat up, losing, and showing up again the next day to do it again.

I learned to find victories where I could. Sometimes it was a victory when I only tapped out (or submitted) one time instead of five. You have to be willing to grind it out and stick with what you love. If you resist the urge to quit, true transformation begins.

That's when I first began to comprehend how discipline creates success. No matter how passionate you are about the *idea* of something, you won't get very far without putting your thoughts into action. Sure, I had a natural aptitude for jiu-jitsu, but if I'd never put in the work and made practicing a priority, I would have remained an average-to-good martial artist at best. Anyone can become great at almost anything if they dedicate enough time and commitment to their chosen task.

Equally important to discipline is faith: believing the path you're following will lead somewhere. I first began teaching classes with Alvis at age seventeen. Teaching with him gave me that first glimpse of what I could become. The more my own practice progressed, the more I could share with others. I fell in love with teaching from the very beginning. Not only was it exciting to see teammates turn my demonstration into actions, but I had to dive even deeper into the techniques myself so that I understood more completely how to teach them to others.

Teaching and training with Alvis, my growth became exponential. I started to understand that I might have found something I could stick with for a very long time. Nothing in school had ever really spoken to me. In fact, I felt itchy and restless even being in school—I was one of those kids who couldn't wait for that 2:30 p.m. dismissal bell every day. As far as extracurricular activities went, I played football for many years, but I just did it because it was something to do. Jiu-jitsu was the first thing to ever really grab me; and the more I sweated on the mat, the stronger my drive to pursue it grew.

Although jiu-jitsu was quickly becoming my sole focus in life, I still imagined a more traditional route for my future. I never really considered college: my brother and I grew up in a single wide trailer at the end of a small trailer park in Tomball, Texas. My family didn't have that much money, and I didn't have the grades or sport accolades to earn any scholarships. I figured my best bet was the military—learning new skills while traveling the world sounded like a good deal to me. Specifically, I fantasized about becoming a Navy SEAL. I couldn't join up until December, so after graduation I got a landscaping job to start saving money, imagining myself bigger and beefier after my SEAL training, wearing camo, hung with gear . . .

But then came an opportunity I couldn't resist. It was one of those moments in life where a pathway opens up in front of you, leading to something that, way up ahead in the distance, looks like it might be your future. In this case, my dad happened to mention that his friend Bradley would be working in Dallas for a few months.

Doesn't sound that earthshaking, right? But it just so happened that Carlos Machado owned a jiu-jitsu school in Dallas. THE Carlos Machado. Considered the father of jiu-jitsu in Texas, Carlos was Alvis's coach and—get this—Chuck Norris's personal martial arts teacher on the set of *Walker, Texas Ranger*. He was also the only jiu-jitsu master within about a thousand miles of me. If Bradley would let me share the room, I could use what I'd saved so far to pay for tuition and cheap food and train under one of the few black belts in the country.

Or I could stick around Houston watering lawns.

I was pretty shy, though, and couldn't work up the nerve to ask Bradley if I could stay with him. I *could*, however, work up the nerve to ask my dad to ask Bradley.

"So Bradley is heading up to Dallas," I said to my dad one night as we sat in front of the TV watching, coincidentally, an episode of *Walker, Texas Ranger*.

"Yep," my dad said (always a man of many words). He didn't turn his head, so I was staring at the salt-and-pepper of his sideburn. "His company's sending him up there on a commercial refrigeration project."

"Cool," I said. "Oh, wow—check that out." Chuck Norris had just choked-out the bad guy. "Um, you know what? The guy who teaches Chuck Norris his jiu-jitsu has a school in Dallas. His name is Carlos Machado."

"Cool," my dad said, eyes glued to the television.

"Well, anyway," I continued, trying to sound as casual as possible. "I'd love to train with Carlos. Do you think Bradley would mind if I asked to stay with him while he's there? So I can take classes?"

This time my dad turned to look at me, surprised. "Well . . . not sure he's got the room, Travis. He's sharing a hotel room with a guy he works with."

"Um, still," I said. I knew my request was starting to sound ridiculous, but I couldn't let this chance slip away. "Would you mind asking him for me?"

One thing I can say about my dad is he's always supported me, even if he didn't always relate to the passion I have for jiu-jitsu. He reached out to Bradley, and incredibly, Bradley and the other guy said I could sleep on the floor of their hotel room. Throw down some blankets for bedding, and I was all set. It was a BIG favor to ask, but I asked, and I'll always be glad I did.

Every day when Bradley and his colleague went off to work, I headed to Carlos's school and trained twice a day: about two hours in the morning, and another one-and-a-half to two-hour class in the evening. Carlos understood the art so well, and his technical proficiency was like none I'd ever experienced. I had seen him in action once when he'd come to Houston to teach a seminar, but nothing compared to being in his presence every day, soaking up every detail. Every class was a new experience. It wasn't just that his moves were so much more technically accurate than anybody else's. It was that he performed them with a Zen-like calm. No matter what position he was in, he never panicked or acted aggressively. His moves were so smooth and seemingly effortless. It was like watching the most graceful and carefully choreographed dance you've ever seen. More than that, there was virtually no ego involved. It was simply jiu-jitsu in its purest form.

For the next four months, at the end of 1999, I returned to the hotel sweaty and exhausted, but filled to capacity with motivation and inspiration. Not only was I learning under one of the most skilled jiu-jitsu masters in the world, but I was also training alongside the best guys in the region.

Carlos Machado presented me with my blue belt in early December. A week later, he offered me an invitation that seemed too good to be true.

"There's a tournament next week at the Gracie Academy in LA. If you're interested in competing, there's a paid-for ticket with your name on it."

I don't think I could have said yes any faster than I did. Since my tenure with Carlos was about to come to an end, I'd been preparing to move back to Houston and enlist in the Navy. But the chance to visit the legendary Gracie Academy was a once-in-a-lifetime opportunity I couldn't pass up.

I can vividly picture walking into the academy. It was huge, super clean, and nice. The entrance showcased a display of Gracie Jiu-Jitsu history, and the people in attendance read like a who's who of jiu-jitsu and MMA. Almost all the competitors were students of either the Gracies or the Machados, with a couple of smaller schools also receiving a few invitations. One of the first people I noticed was the legend himself, Hélio Gracie—the cofounder (and veritable godfather) of Brazilian Jiu-Jitsu. He must have been in his mid-eighties then, short but lean and erect, with the high-cheekboned face of a hawk. He and his brother Carlos were the reason I was there. Together they created Gracie Jiu-Jitsu, which became known as Brazilian Jiu-Jitsu. I remember feeling numb and tingly as I got to say hello and shake his hand.

Other attendees included Hélio's son and jiu-jitsu pioneer, Royce Gracie; Ed O'Neill, the actor known as Al Bundy from *Married with Children*, an early devotee of the art; Travis "Serial Killer" Lutter; Robert DeFranco; Rico Rodriguez; and Anthony Perosh—all stalwart competitors and champions of jiu-jitsu and the UFC. Even Rafael Lovato Jr was there. Only sixteen years old at the time, Rafael would go on to be the winningest American in jiu-jitsu history. He is currently the Bellator Middleweight World Champion. In other words, the competitors in attendance were of world-class caliber.

This event was unlike any I had competed in before. There were no time limits. Matches were won in one of two ways: by submission or by being the first to score fifteen points. The rest of that trip was a blur because I had only one match, but it was a doozy and it took everything I had.

I squared off on the mat against another, more seasoned blue belt. The match started, and I was able to secure a takedown and a guard pass to gain a few points early. "Okay, this shouldn't be too bad," I probably thought to myself. "Time to press ahead, and I'll get the submission in no time."

But "no time" turned into five minutes, and then twelve minutes. My opponent kept escaping my control and recovering his guard. I started feeling wiped. He hadn't scored any points on me. We'd scramble and

I'd pass his guard, but he would recover. Twelve minutes became twenty, then thirty, then forty minutes. My head was light, I was soaked in sweat, my throat was on fire for a drop of water, and I could barely keep my hands in front of me. I had gotten to twelve points. My opponent still had zero. I was almost guaranteed the win, but I had to either get him to submit—unlikely, given my weakened state—or score three more points. My opponent didn't look so hot either. It probably looked like a bar fight between two wasted barflies by the end.

I glanced at the referee and thought, "Okay, if I just pass his guard one more time, I'll get the three points needed." I wasn't going to quit just because I wanted to lie down and die. I was in it to win. I made one more scramble, got past his guard, and held him in place to secure the points. I smiled: thank God it was over.

Except the referee didn't give me the points. I remember looking at him like, *Motherfucker, really? I had him!* My teammates were also vocal about the non-call. The referee wouldn't have it. No points awarded.

By this point, I'm not even sure how I'm still breathing. Is it considered submission if I just collapse? I wasn't sure. I gave it one more try. I loosened my control and my opponent recovered guard. I immediately passed his guard for the final time, and then, with the last sip of energy in my muscles, I held and glared at the referee.

The referee stood with arms akimbo, leaning in as if he wasn't sure. It seemed to take forever for him to decide, but he finally did. After forty-five minutes of fighting, he finally gave me my last points, and I collapsed on the mat and literally crawled back to my team. I had never been that exhausted before, and I've never been since.

I'm not sure how, but I made it back to the apartment I was sharing with my team. I remember that a bunch of the guys were going out drinking after the tournament. I was too young to drink, but I didn't want to go anyway. I just slept on the couch the whole time. But I had won and in the company of some of the most awesome names in the sport. Many of the details of that day might have escaped me, but I'll never forget the exhaustion—and I'll never forget shaking Hélio's hand.

Following My Purpose

Reaching a goal like a blue belt feels great, but that feeling actually fades pretty fast. It's pursuing the goal that makes martial arts fulfilling—just like life. Renew your goals constantly and pursue them with all you've got—that's how you find purpose in what you do. Many religions will label purpose as living for God or gods. Family will sometimes try to define your purpose for you by insisting that you follow in a parent's footsteps. Others will see a talent you have and try to give you a purpose based on this talent.

But don't try to make everyone happy. You will only succeed in being less happy yourself. Ultimately, you must create your own purpose or "destiny." I found that out myself when I got back from Dallas and got ready to enlist in the Navy.

I'd completed all of the necessary applications and was cleared except for a final medical examination. By this time I'd been training a lot and was in really great shape. The medical exam would be easy peasy . . . or so I thought. Somewhere in the time between my stay in Dallas and returning home, I'd developed eczema on my right ring finger, just a little rash, probably from an allergic reaction. Barely seems worth mentioning, right? Well, in my case, this mild condition raised some kind of red flag during the exam. So on my ship-out day, I was not allowed to ship out. To get into the Navy, I'd need a waiver.

It seemed ridiculous—come on, eczema couldn't keep me out of the Navy! But the longer I waited in limbo, the more worried I got. It was probably about a month, but it seemed like two or three before the phone rang with the final decision.

"Hey man," the guy on the other end said. "Bad news. The waiver was rejected."

"Okay," I said slowly, trying to figure out what exactly this meant. "I got the right medicine, and the eczema is totally gone now. Do I have to re-apply, or what do I do?"

"No. Unfortunately, it means you can't go at all," he said matter-of-factly. "You've been denied. But here's the good news: you can go into the Army instead, but it will be with a different job and at a lower starting rank."

As we continued to talk, I quickly worked out what *that* meant. I'd be enlisting in a different branch of the military, I wouldn't get to choose the job I wanted, and I'd be entering at the lowest level.

Nothing about that felt right. It didn't even come close to fulfilling any plan I'd had for myself. "I'll think about it," I said. "But I don't think that's going to work for me."

I placed the cordless phone back down on the charger and stood there for a moment, taking in what had just happened. I had no idea what I was going to do. I didn't feel heartbroken, exactly, but I did feel very lost. I knew I could still figure out a course for my life. I was smart, I had drive, and because of jiu-jitsu I wasn't afraid of hard work. I just wasn't sure exactly which path to focus on next. My mental map of the next four years had been wiped clean.

I needed a new plan. So much of what happens to you is out of your control and even random, but so what. As a martial artist and as an entrepreneur, I've learned that when your plan doesn't work, it's not time to give up. It's time to make an adjustment. I had a handful of private students at Alvis's school and remained committed to my training. That hadn't changed. All I needed was a part-time income to supplement what I made at the studio. A plan would come to me soon—and maybe, just maybe, it would have something to do with jiu-jitsu.

So I found a job as a personal trainer at 24 Hour Fitness, and the extra income and flexibility allowed me to continue pursuing my goals in jiu-jitsu. In fact, I purposely scheduled all of my personal training clients between two and six p.m. so that I could still get in two-a-days at the academy. I probably could have made more money by setting up appointments when people were actually NOT at work, but there was only so much of my own day I was willing to sacrifice. Though I loved training people, I didn't have passion for the work. I knew I wanted to master and teach jiu-jitsu, so I wasn't going to allow my training to suffer.

For the next four years, when I wasn't working for someone else (24 Hour Fitness and a brief stint for UPS), I dedicated every spare minute to elevating my own skills and sharing everything I knew with the students. I continued to travel to Dallas to train under Carlos Machado and eventually earned my brown belt in 2002.

• • •

Once you start sharing more and giving back, it changes the way you view your purpose. This is a huge part of being a martial artist, as opposed to simply "somebody taking a martial arts class." It's also what distinguishes an inspirational leader from a mere boss. Purpose almost always involves sharing your passion with a community. Without it, you quickly lose sight of why you were pursuing your passion in the first place.

In fact, two students I trained, Will and Brandon Lorenz, ended up helping to set me on the next path of my jiu-jitsu journey, perhaps the most transformative path of all. More specifically, it was their father, Bill Lorenz, who presented me with the kind of gift you can never repay but are forever grateful for.

I had trained Will and Brandon on and off for several years alongside Alvis. They were two of the best kids in the country, doing judo, wrestling, and jiu-jitsu and winning nearly every competition they entered. Will, the older, was quiet and controlled; Brandon was a physical and emotional firecracker. Bill really liked my teaching style, which was focused on highly technical and accurate application of the art, and appreciated the way I worked with both of them. My love and passion for jiu-jitsu always came through when I was working with his boys. And although Bill would often ask about my goals and ambitions, one day he caught me off guard.

He invited me to lunch and got blunt. "Why aren't you in Brazil, man?" he asked me without warning. Bill was a child of the '60s. He had shoulder-length white hair, always wore sandals, was a smooth guitar player, and was about as cool as they come.

The question surprised me so much I straightened up to look at him. "What do you mean?" The thought of going to Brazil had never really crossed my mind. It simply wasn't reasonable. When you've never had money, it never even occurs to you to spend time dreaming up far-fetched ideas like that one. "Move to Brazil? I don't see how I could do that."

"I'd be happy to try to make this a possibility if you're interested," he said. The restaurant crowd thinned out as the lunch hour winded down. "Think it over. I think it would be the right move for you. I see the way you work with my boys. You're a great teacher and you've got lot to offer." Will and Brandon had just finished eating, and Brandon started putting Will in a mock choke-hold. Bill laughed as he separated them. "Knock it off, buddy." Then he looked at me. "Honestly, Travis. I think Brazil is the next logical step."

It was one of those life-changing turning points, one that I completely failed to notice. In the weeks to come, I barely gave the conversation a second thought. The fact was, at that time, my goal was to continue to work with Alvis both as an instructor and a partial business partner. My friend Jeremy Trahan introduced me to some motivational reading material. I'd been reading a lot of Tony Robbins's books, and I was really excited about the idea of becoming an entrepreneur. I had finally come up with a new plan for myself after being rejected from the Navy, and my mind was pretty set.

Until a couple of months later, that is, when Alvis and I traveled to the world championships in Brazil and did some training there. From the moment I got off the plane in Rio, I had a gut feeling that this place was pretty special. Between the tournament, the training, and the people, it was the exact opposite feeling I'd gotten when I'd been presented with the idea of going into the Army. It felt *right*.

The next time I saw him back in Houston, Bill and I were watching Brandon practice in class. "How was training in Brazil?" he asked.

"It. Was. Awesome," I said, emphasizing every word and making direct eye contact with Bill. "Really, really awesome. Really great. Just . . . awesome."

Yeah, I was at a loss for words. Now that I'd experienced it firsthand, I was desperate to get back to Brazil. But somehow I didn't want to ask Bill outright if his offer was still on the table. I guess I hoped that repeating "awesome" over and over combined with some pleading glances would be enough of a hint.

"That's good to hear," Bill said, patting my shoulder and grinning from ear to ear. "I told you you'd love it." He turned back to watching Brandon, and in the ensuing silence, broken only by the grunts of the boys on the mat, my heart sank.

"The thing of it is, Bill . . ." I started, unsure of how to ask my generous friend for help. "What I mean to say—"

"My offer still stands, you know," he said glancing back at me. "I mean, if you're thinking about going back."

In that moment, a whole new world of possibilities opened up for me. Not only was I being given the opportunity to live in Brazil and train with some of the greatest Brazilian Jiu-Jitsu fighters on the planet, but I was confident that my newly acquired skills would pave the way for me to open my own academy when I returned.

Within a few months from that turning-point conversation, I was on the plane. And my dad had already given his blessing to use his garage to teach jiu-jitsu lessons when I got back.

Sometimes the less you know, the less you fear. I'd never left Texas for longer than two weeks, I didn't speak a word of Portuguese, I didn't know a single soul in Brazil, and I had no idea how much money it would take to live on once I got there. All I could do was work with what I'd been given and trust that this leap of faith would show me where I needed to go next.

Humans don't mind hardship, in fact they thrive on it; what they mind is not feeling necessary. Modern society has perfected the art of making people not feel necessary.

—Sebastian Junger[4]

It won't be [easy] ... You are not rewarded for the comfortable choice.

—Aubrey Marcus[5]

CHAPTER 2

Faith and Fortitude

Bem vindo ao Brasil

Honking horns. Thick tropical air. Clouds of smoke billowing from dangling exhaust pipes as taxis dart in and out of traffic in search of fares.

And words. So many words.

"*Ei!*"

"*Oi!*"

"*Tudo bem?*"

"*Com licença!*"

"*Olá!*"

"*Por aqui!*"

"*Porra, Caralho!*"

Officers shouting directions. People hailing taxis. Folks flagging down loved ones. Portuguese phrases punctuated the air around me at a rapid-fire pace, swirling around my brain as I weaved around the maze of

---

4   Sebastian Junger, *Tribe: On Homecoming and Belonging* (New York: Hatchett Book Group, 2016), xvii.

5   Aubrey Marcus, *Own the Day, Own Your Life: Optimized Practices for Waking, Working, Learning, Eating, Training, Playing, Sleeping, and Sex* (New York: HarperCollins, 2017), 49.

suitcases and moved further along the curb outside the airport. After months of preparation, I had arrived in Rio de Janeiro.

It had been nearly six months since I'd been to Brazil for the world championships, and this time promised to be a much different experience.

First and foremost, there's a huge contrast between *visiting* someplace and *living* there. Also, I was alone, so I didn't have the benefit of a friendly face or a translator. And finally, while I had enough of a plan to get myself started in a new country, I'd need to reassess and adjust once I settled in. Between the $500-per-month allowance that Bill had provided and the $1,500 I'd sold my car for, I had about $30 a day to live on (roughly 80 Brazilian reals) for the next three months—including rent, food, jiu-jitsu training, everything.

My first splurge was going to be on a taxi; no way was I ready to figure out the bus system just yet. My immediate goal was much simpler: Make it to Barra da Tijuca, which was about forty-five minutes southwest of Galeão International Airport (GIA), using the handful of Portuguese phrases I'd been practicing for this very purpose. I knew the name of the hostel (or *pousada*) where I was staying, I knew the name of the town where it was located (I'd been to the area the previous year), and I knew how to say things like "Keep going straight." I was as ready as I was ever going to be.

I spotted a taxi, slid into the backseat, and said as clearly as I possibly could: *"Leve-me para Barra."*

The cab lurched forward, squeezing in between cars and maneuvering into an opening that seemed barely big enough for a tricycle, much less a compact car. Everywhere around us, cars battled for the precious real estate between bumper-to-bumper buses and careening motorcycles. In Rio, if you follow traffic laws and drive carefully, you will piss other drivers off and cause accidents. The only "safe" way to drive is adhering to the same level of organized chaos everyone else does.

The moment we exited the airport, my eyes were glued to the landscape. Brazil is a country of juxtapositions. You land in a congested city just pumping out pollution, and a few minutes later, you'll pass lush, emerald-green rainforest and mile-long beaches with peacock-blue waves lapping the shore. In some areas, mountainsides are dominated by armies of the orangish-red concrete houses that signal the country's most impoverished areas, known as *favelas*. The bigger favelas may contain well over one hundred thousand people. Homes are stacked so tightly and built at such haphazard angles that the entire area resembles a shantytown made from an incomplete set of Legos. Laundry lines zig-zag between buildings like colorful flags, stringing everything together. Ironically, in their extreme poverty, many people who live in favelas often enjoy the best ocean views Brazil has to offer.

On the flip side, extravagant gated communities—like any upscale development in a US suburb—often sit just a short drive from these massive favelas, sharing the same seaside views.

While I sat back taking everything in, I kept my eyes peeled for familiar landmarks. As we approached Barra, I began to direct the cab driver through the congested streets clogged with cars, pedestrians, and cyclists, using a combination of very basic Portuguese and directional hand gestures. By the time we arrived at the Pousada Barra Sol, I was dog-tired.

At the simple yet clean hostel, I gave my first week's rent of $140 to the brunette proprietress, who happily accepted my American currency. I dragged my suitcase down the hallway and into my room and collapsed on the twin bed. After spending eight sleepless hours on the red-eye flight from Houston, I was ready to lay down and sleep for as long as my body would let me.

A Small Fish in a Big Pond

That first morning I woke up with my body craving more sleep, but the rest of me was pumped and ready to begin training. I decided on the thirty-minute walk to class, so I didn't have to pay for a taxi. I stepped outside and the heat punched me in the face. It was like a sauna, and that means something coming from a guy raised in Houston. I was dripping wet by the time I arrived at the right address. Oh yeah, I had two flights of stairs to climb, no biggie. When I finally reached class, I realized another thing I had forgotten from my previous trip—no AC, only fans. That's one thing I knew I'd miss. I was already a ball of sweat and class hadn't started. This was going to be fun.

It was soon evident that despite my BJJ acumen back home, I still had a lot to learn. In fact, on my very first day of class, I had barely taken my place on the mat when my black belt opponent passed my guard, wrapped my arm with my own gi (what I now like to call "the sling"), and submitted me with a collar choke (or a "paper cutter"). I had never seen this variation of the choke before, so there was no way I could defend myself against it.

And yet in the split second before I grabbed my partner's outstretched hand to get back up, I was awash in triumph. One day in class, and I was already encountering never-before-seen moves! Any lingering doubts I had about whether I'd made the right decision to come to Brazil were obliterated. This was the start of something special.

For the first couple of weeks, my days consisted of nothing more than waking up, heading to the Gracie Barra Jiu-Jitsu Academy, and returning to the pousada to shower off the stink before collapsing into bed. As a Houston native, I was pretty used to dealing with heat, but summertime in Brazil was astounding. Not only was I walking for thirty minutes through sticky, steamy air to get to the gym, but I would then walk up two flights of stairs to train in an unair-conditioned room equipped only with a couple of tiny fans that barely stirred the air. If it was 100 degrees outside (and it often was), it felt more like 125 inside. When the windows were open, there *might* be a gust of wind, but for the most part I could barely spar for two or three rounds before I felt like I might pass out. It was like doing extreme sports in a sauna, but fully dressed in a gi.

After class, I'd sometimes go to lunch or hang out with some of the guys from the academy, but that could get kind of frustrating. Most of the gym instructors spoke English, and there were enough foreigners in class that language was never a barrier. But socializing with locals outside the gym was a different matter. The majority of my "conversation" skills boiled down to me nodding along and interjecting *"Ta bem"* or *"Ta bom"* when there was a lull, which is sort of like saying "It's all good," "Uh huh," or the ever-compelling and insightful "Mmm-hmm." Generic as these phrases are, it was better than repeating *"Eu não entendo"* ("I don't understand what you're saying") over and over, which I discovered was a real conversation killer. I figured it was better to keep the conversation going as long as possible so I had a shot at absorbing something.

Even more frustrating were the mishaps that could happen when I was ordering food. Sometimes I'd be served a super greasy salami (*salame*) sandwich instead of the fresh, healthy salmon (*salmão*) I thought I'd ordered, and I had no way of fixing it because I didn't know enough words to tell the server it was a mistake.

Between the exhaustion of training in a boiling hot gym and the exasperation of trying to communicate every time I left my room, most days I simply chose to return to the pousada and study Portuguese.

Back home, the jiu-jitsu pool was so small that I'd been one of the top competitors in the area, but now that I was training with the best guys in the world at one of the most successful jiu-jitsu academies in the history of the sport, I was outside my comfort zone and realizing how little I knew. While it was exhilarating to be studying under the masters, I also felt humbled and intimidated by being a "newbie" again. I held my own against other brown belts, but many of the black belts put me in my place almost every time.

One day when I was walking home along the heavily trafficked Avenida das Americas, a plain-looking economy car—one that kind of looked like the car I'd driven in Houston as a teen, except the rolled-up windows suggested that this one had AC—pulled up beside me. Brazilian music cut through the dense air as the man inside rolled down his window.

"Hey, bro, you need a ride?" he asked in thickly accented English.

I did a double take. The voice belonged to none other than Royler Gracie, a four-time black belt world champion and one of the founding fathers of Brazilian Jiu-Jitsu. Not only was this legend offering me a ride, but he apparently knew who I was. I'd seen him drop by the Gracie Barra academy here and there, but he was never training so it didn't occur to me that he'd noticed me.

To a jiu-jitsu nerd like me, this was the equivalent of Tom Hanks or Meryl Streep approaching a young unknown actor on the street. Obviously, I accepted the offer.

Once I hopped in and got situated, trying my best not to spread my sweat around his front seat, he said, "You hungry? I was just about to grab a bite to eat."

"Sure . . ." I said with slight hesitation, working out how to bring up the fact that I didn't have any money on me. I had counted on eating back at the pousada, where a pretty decent-sized meal cost about R5$ (about $1.75), which was about all I could afford.

"My treat," he added in the nick of time, saving me from having to respond further.

I didn't care that my gi was stiff with dried sweat or that my hair was shellacked to my head from perspiration. I had been in Brazil only a matter of weeks, and I was going to lunch with Royler Gracie!

After a short drive, we turned onto a side street and pulled up at an outdoor café with plastic tables and chairs on a wooden deck lined with decorative palm trees. It was surprisingly quiet considering it was only a couple of blocks in from the hustle and bustle of the Avenida.

Once our orders had been placed and our water glasses filled, Royler leaned back with a smile. "How's it going at Barra?" he said with a smooth Brazilian accent. His body was short and lean, but under his close-cropped black hair he had wide-set brown eyes and a friendly grin.

"Not bad," I said. "I'm definitely learning a lot. I mean, I knew I was coming down here to get to the next level, but I don't think I realized how many levels there really are. The guys I train with are incredible."

"Yeah," he said. "Tough to feel like you're learning all over again. But it'll make you a better fighter, man. Keep at it, every day, and remember to keep your emotions under control, even on the toughest days."

"Well, thanks for that," I said. "I'm not sure if I'm actually controlling my emotions on the mat, or if it's just that I am too beat-down from the heat to get all worked up."

"I hear you," he said with a laugh. "Summer in Rio—oof. And you came down here by yourself?"

"Yep," I said.

"What do you think of Brazil?" he said. "Other than the heat."

"Oh, Brazil is awesome," I said. "I still can't believe I'm here. The beaches are beautiful, and the women are amazing. It's unbelievable."

"Yes, well, Brazil does have its perks," Royler said, clearly amused by my very touristy description of his country. "But be careful. Brazil also has a dark side. Watch your back when you're walking around. There's a lot of thieves and pickpockets out there, and a lot of the police are corrupt. How old are you? Twenty? Twenty-one?"

"Twenty-two," I said.

"Wow," he said. "Big step, coming down to Brazil on your own, twenty-two years old. I like that. I like motivation and discipline in a young guy. I don't see it so much these days."

"I knew I had to come back after going to the world championship last year," I replied. "It just took me a while to figure out how I was going to do it."

"Good decision, man," he said. A moped sputtered past. "You'll never regret it, I promise you that."

Our plates had arrived, piled high with mountains of rice and beans and a thick strip of grilled beef. Desperate for post-training carbs, I scooped up a forkful while still trying to get the juice out of every precious moment with Royler. "So, what do you have coming up?" I said, trying not to talk with my mouth full. "When's your next competition?"

"Good question, my friend," he said. His eyes followed a taxi down the street and around a corner. "Not really sure. Trying to figure a few things out. Getting sponsorship is not so easy, and a lot of MMA organizations, they don't pay very well."

This was shocking. Not only was Royler a jiu-jitsu world champion and MMA champion, but his renowned Gracie Humaitá Academy, located just outside of Rio, had produced some of the sport's biggest names, including Saulo and Xande Ribeiro, each of whom laid claim to several world titles. Still, he struggled to make a decent living as a martial artist. Sometimes we build up star athletes as if they are superhuman, but having lunch with Royler that day reminded me that every one of us has our own challenges to overcome.

More than that, I saw that without the proper support systems in place, talent will only take you so far. I found myself silently thanking Bill for the support he'd offered me. The revelation also confirmed my belief that I needed to continue creating a solid business plan once I got back to the US. If I wanted to turn jiu-jitsu into a full-fledged career, I had to make sure I was building a rock-solid foundation for my future that wasn't reliant on the ebb and flow of the sport's popularity.

The lunch crowd was beginning to thin out. We scraped up the last bits of rice on our plates, and Royler asked for the check.

"Thanks again for lunch," I said. "I really appreciate it."

"No problem, bro. Keep training hard," he said with a smile.

Striking Out on My Own

After a few weeks, it was time to move out of the pousada. I had $750 to live on per month and that included *everything*, so spending $600 of that on room and board wasn't a good idea. A friend I knew from the States, Scott "Scotty" Nelson (owner of the famed Brazilian Jiu-Jitsu apparel company/website On the Mat), had a condo and rented out rooms. I spent a week living in a room about five feet by ten feet (or roughly the size of a closet) while I figured out where to go next. Though the room was small, the condo itself was located in a nice suburbanesque neighborhood in Barra surrounded by other condo communities. It was the kind of place I could have easily gotten used to—but it was only slightly more affordable than the pousada, so I couldn't stay for long.

Not much was available on my penny-pinching budget, but then I got lucky. Another guy training at the academy, Dennis Asche, had his own place and offered me a room for R$750 a month (around $250 US), including my own bathroom. Dennis's place was located on Ilha Primeira, a small island on the Canal da Barra da Tijuca that was only accessible by ferry. Even factoring in the cost of ferry rides—which ranged between .50c to R$1, depending where you were going—the rent was financially sustainable. The two-story house was about six hundred square feet, one hundred square feet of which was my room. It came with a mattress that sat on a frame so low to the ground it might as well have been on the floor. That left plenty of room for the two suitcases I'd brought with me.

Even though the house was smaller than what I was used to back home, I found the pace of the island itself soothing. Everyone knew one another, and though it was just a short boat ride to the mainland, it felt laid back and secluded.

Dennis loaned me a TV about the size of a laptop, but since there was no television service, I had my choice of watching either *Lord of the Rings* or *Snatch*, both of which Dennis owned on VHS. I watched each movie about twenty-seven times (I'm pretty sick of *Lord of the Rings* to this day, but *Snatch* is still awesome). They weren't developing my language skills any, but it was cheap entertainment for the first couple of months.

I did have an English-Portuguese pocket dictionary, and Dennis loaned me a copy of *501 Portuguese Verbs*, so I continued making minor strides in learning Portuguese. But I still felt like my brain was broken when I was out and about. Beyond basic small talk and ordering food, I was pretty limited.

One Saturday night I was on my way home from a friend's house at about midnight and accidentally got on the wrong bus. I had never been to this part of town before (somewhere northwest of Barra), so I wasn't sure how to get back. My friend had told me which bus to take, but I guess I forgot the number.

Eventually, I realized the bus wasn't heading toward Barra. I rang the bell so I could get off and try to find the right bus home. The driver pulled over, and I stepped out into the heat and darkness of the summer night. I had no idea where I was, but I knew it didn't feel right. I heard the clink of a glass bottle skipping across the sidewalk and a distant altercation muffled by the close-knit buildings, which all had window bars and metal armor decorated in graffiti covering the door. This was nothing like Barra, nothing like the town I had left just a few minutes before. This was a favela.

A friendly-looking older lady was walking along the street, so I decided to ask for help. *"Desculpe-me senhora,"* I said. *"Qual bairro e esse?"*

"Cidade de Deus," she replied.

"Ah, *obrigado,"* I replied faintly. I couldn't believe it. I had landed smack-dab in the center of Cidade de Deus, one of the most violent favelas in Brazil and the inspiration behind the 2002 film *City of God*. As I stood there on the sidewalk trying to figure out what to do next, I had a vision of being swarmed by hordes of gun-toting delinquents. I had heard and read so much about the dangers of going into these neighborhoods, especially at night. Rival gang violence and drug deals gone wrong were commonplace. My thoughts were as follows: (1) I can't speak Portuguese very well; (2) I don't have enough cash for a taxi; and (3) I'm going to be murdered for my sneakers.

I took a few tentative steps down the dimly lit street. The sounds of Saturday night surrounded me: clinking beer bottles, raucous laughter, street vendors selling homemade desserts. So far, so good. Nobody was pointing and shouting *"Pegue o gringo!"* ("Grab the foreigner!") The few street lamps that weren't blown out cast long shadows down otherwise dark alleyways, illuminating stray dogs rooting around discarded to-go containers and cigarette butts. I fixed an expression on my face that I hoped conveyed "Don't mess with me, I am a hardened criminal, and if you come near me, something bad is going to happen to you." Hunching my shoulders, I strode purposefully toward the next stop, taking care not to make eye contact with anyone I passed, at least if I could help it. A middle-aged man who looked like he'd seen better days tumbled out of a doorway and gave me a strange look. I yanked my hands out of my pockets and balled them up in fists at my side, preparing for fight or flight. Whether it was my intimidating stance or that he was seeing two of me through an alcohol-induced haze, I'll never know. He moved on quickly, and I did the same.

I had to wait a bit for the bus, which didn't help ease my discomfort, as I was growing more nervous by the minute. The longer I stood there waiting, the more anxious I became. When the bus finally arrived and the doors pushed open, I stepped up with one foot, but left the other firmly on the pavement.

"*Este ônibus vai para barra?*" I said to the driver. I didn't want to stay any longer than necessary, but I also didn't want to make a mistake and end up in another sketchy area.

"*O que?*" he said, clearly not comprehending my butchered version of his language.

"*ESTE ONIBUS VAI PARA BARRA?*" I replied hoping that speaking louder would get my message across.

"*Ah, Barra!*" he said. "*Sim, sim. Nós estamos indo para barra. Venha, venha.*"

I wasn't entirely sure what every word he said meant, but I understood "Barra" and "yes," so I got on and grabbed an empty seat close to the front. For the entire ride home, I was on the lookout for signs that indicated we were getting closer to Barra. Much to my relief, within thirty minutes we were back in town.

"*Obrigado,*" I said, thanking the driver as I stepped down from the bus.

He lifted two fingers off the steering wheel in a weary wave and replied, "*Boa sorte.*" Good luck.

• • •

My misstep with the bus didn't deter me from continuing to explore on my own. One of my favorite pastimes was hiking Pedra da Gavea, a granite mountain located in the Tijuca Forest that reaches 844 meters and drops down directly into the Atlantic Ocean. The starting point of the climb was only a thirty-minute walk from where I lived, but when I was up there, I felt like I was the only person in the world. As I trekked, I'd imagine I was experiencing Brazil the way it was hundreds of years ago, before industrialization dug in its sharp claws. No houses, no people: just waterfalls, monkeys, sloths, giant lizards, croaking toucans, mammoth jackfruit trees (even though they actually came from Asia), and that pure rainforest smell.

The fresh, earthy scent was a stark contrast to the stench that wafted off the canal on days when sewage was released in the Canal da Barra, or the pungent odor of public urination, a funk that could make a coroner wretch once Carnaval kicked into full gear. Carnaval, Brazil's version of Mardi Gras, is a six-day festival that ends on Ash Wednesday. Over the course of those days, hundreds of tourists from around the globe descend upon Brazil to join the locals in blowing off steam before the onset of Lent. It's nothing short of bacchanalian—drinking, drugs, dancing, debauchery—and let's just say that taking time out from the revelry to find an actual restroom is not always a top priority when nature calls.

The huge influx of tourists (and their wallets) also attracts an increased number of prostitutes. I had seen these women around town, but during Carnaval it seemed like every woman on Copacabana Beach was of the "working" variety. I was constantly approached by beautiful women, and not because I'm so damn attractive and charming, but because I was clearly American, and they probably assumed I was there for a "good time." I'd be sitting outside on the boardwalk with friends when a drop-dead gorgeous woman would stop by the table and invite herself to sit down. Initially I had no idea these were "working" women. I just thought I'd stumbled into the ultimate paradise. We would talk, chat, flirt, and have perfectly normal and engaging conversations. The more women I chatted with, the better my Portuguese got.

Usually the dream abruptly ended when a proposal was made and declined—not really my thing. Plus, I really thought they liked me, so I was a bit butthurt. However, some chose to continue hanging out, even after I made it clear that I wasn't interested in their "offer." These conversations, which shed a lot of light on Brazilian culture, were the most memorable to me. In addition, they really helped with my Portuguese. After these heart-to-hearts, it was impossible for me to look at these women in the same way. Some of them had never known another way of life, and this was a means of survival for them.

In fact, years later I was giving a walking tour of Copacabana for a friend who was visiting from the States. It wasn't Carnaval, but there were still plenty of girls trying to make money off tourists. As we threaded in and out of the ever-present throngs of people, my friend came to a dead stop and grabbed my arm.

"Hey, bro," he said. "Did you see that?"

"See what?" I said.

"Over there, that girl," he said, gesturing toward a scantily dressed woman. "And over there, too."

"Well," I said, turning to look at him. "If you think they're hookers, then, yes, you're exactly right."

"There's so many of them!" he said.

"Yeah?" I said, unsure where he was going with the conversation.

"How can they be okay with being hookers?" he said. "How can you just wake up one day and say, 'I'm gonna start banging ten guys a day for a living'? It's disgusting!"

"Hey man, listen," I said, continuing down the street so we weren't clogging the sidewalk. "You don't know anything about that person. So don't judge them."

"Well, I know enough to know that they have no values if they're doing that every day," he retorted. "They have no interest in holding a real job, and this is easy money. It's gross."

"Wow," I said. Now it was my turn to come to a dead stop. "You really have no idea, do you? For all you know, this girl comes from a favela, has never met her father, was born addicted to drugs, and her drug-addicted mother is also a prostitute. This may be the only way she's ever been able to feed herself and her family."

"Are you kidding me?" he said "Are you actually telling me that you believe there's no other way she can make money? I find that really hard to believe."

"That's because you're a privileged American who has never missed a meal in his entire life," I said, stepping around him to press the button for the crosswalk. "You don't know what it feels like to be hungry, sad, and addicted to drugs with only yourself to rely on. You've been given every opportunity to thrive. Meanwhile, this girl spends her days just trying to survive." A taxi went careening past, and I stepped back automatically. I was sweating, and not just because it was a warm evening. "It's tragic and it's sad, but it's true. For some of these girls, this is the only life they've known since they were nine years old. Don't jump to conclusions and assume that they just woke up one day and decided to be a prostitute. The truth is, if you had her parents, her genetics, and her exact life circumstance, you'd be the one turning tricks for money. Believe whatever you want, man, but it's true."

His eyes got big and he stopped talking. For the next few blocks, we walked in silence. I hoped he was taking my words to heart and that Brazil was expanding his mind the way it had mine.

Tchau for Now

Despite the helpful working girls, I had been in Brazil for nearly three months, and I was still befuddled by Portuguese. I got to the point where I thought I might have to admit that maybe I just didn't have it in me to learn another language. No matter how much I practiced, I still felt alone at a table crowded with people laughing and gesturing with their pão de queijo and talking a mile a minute, with me barely able to catch a familiar word here and there. The worst part was that because I knew *some* words and spoke with a decent accent, people spoke to me more rapidly and in slang. When I didn't respond in kind, they assumed I was shy or, worse, rude.

Just when I was ready to throw in the towel, I had a small but significant mental breakthrough. I had been dating a girl for a couple of weeks (me muddling through with my piss-poor Portuguese, and she speaking what little English she knew), and she took me to a restaurant with a few of her friends. I'll never forget the feeling of complete incompetence while sitting at that table. The fast-talking, slang-infused conversation left me feeling that I had no business trying to learn Portuguese.

I guess one of them noticed my awkward silence and decided to involve me in the conversation. I didn't understand what he asked me; I just recall the fear I felt when everyone turned to hear my reply.

"*Como?*" I replied as I steeled myself to admit to him that I couldn't understand what he was saying.

"*Voce esta gostando do Brasil?*" he repeated, looking at me expectantly.

I understood this time—"Are you liking Brazil?"—and responded with a brief "*Sim.*"

I considered leaving it at that to avoid the embarrassment of stumbling through more small talk. But something inside compelled me to press on.

"*Brasil e muito legal. Eu gusto,*" I said. ("Brazil is very cool. I like it.")

After that, even though I had trouble understanding a lot of what was said, I kept trying. After all, if Brazil had taught me nothing else, it was that you can't allow fear to prevent you from trying new things. Even when you fail (and everybody fails at some point when testing out new territory), nobody is going to remember for very long. Everyone is too busy worrying about their own mistakes and insecurities to spend much time worrying about yours, so you might as well put yourself out there.

It doesn't matter if you're mastering jiu-jitsu or a new language, the process is similar. You learn specific techniques (or words and phrases) and a certain number of techniques (or grammatical rules), but in the end, there are endless ways to blend everything together. You just have to commit to the process long enough to grasp the fundamentals, and you have to keep practicing even if it feels like you're making a fool of yourself.

Before I first visited Brazil, the farthest I'd traveled away from home was a three-day trip to California for competition. Now I was learning a new language in a city nearly five thousand miles from where I grew up and training in the motherland of jiu-jitsu. I just had to figure out how to make this journey last a little bit longer. My visa was about to expire, but I wasn't done with Brazil just yet. I was just getting started.

If we possess our why of life we can put up with almost any how.

—Friedrich Nietzsche[6]

Vulnerability is not knowing victory or defeat, it's understanding the necessity of both; it's engaging. It's being all in.

—Dr. Brené Brown[7]

CHAPTER 3

Leaps and Love

The Power of "Why"

Whether you've been studying martial arts for a while, building a business, or pursuing a worthwhile goal, you almost certainly know that anything worth doing takes time and commitment. It requires sweat, sometimes blood, and always some tears. You have to know *why* you're doing what you're doing, or you won't stick with it. There needs to be a compelling reason to keep you going past the setbacks and difficulties. I had a compelling reason—my *why*—for studying BJJ.

In order to achieve a measure of success in anything, you must embrace the uncomfortable. As you push yourself beyond the anxiety and discomfort, they become more comfortable. New experiences change you, expand your mind, and challenge you to grow. One idea will spark the next idea. For me, I knew why I was investing all of this time, energy, money, and focus into jiu-jitsu. It was not only my passion—it was my dream to get really good at the art and one day turn teaching into my

---

6   Friedrich Nietzsche, *Twilight of the Idols*, in *Twilight of the Idols and The Anti-Christ*, trans. R. J. Hollingdale (London: Penguin, 1990), 33.

7   Brené Brown, Ph.D., LMSW, *Daring Greatly: How the Courage to Be Vulnerable Transforms the Way We Live, Love, Parent and Lead* (New York: Penguin, 2015), 2.

profession and livelihood. That's what kept me going. That's why I took leaps into the unknown. I was willing to make the mistakes and fail so that I could learn.

Without a strong why, a purpose, the desire to continue on will perish and you will likely quit. You'll give up at the first signs of failure. That uncompromising level of commitment is what it takes to become a black belt in any discipline.

Learning Portuguese, on the other hand, was a different matter. I had found a Portuguese-to-English dictionary, a book called *501 Portuguese Verbs*, and had made some flash cards, but studying them all felt tedious. And after a long day on the mat, trying to keep up with a rapid-fire conversation about the fate of the Flamengo *futebol* club was just too much, too hard. And frankly it was embarrassing that I had to constantly ask shop clerks, waiters, and fellow students, "*Fale mais devagar, por favor*" ("Please speak more slowly"). Sure, I liked the idea of learning a second language, but I also knew I could get by without having to learn it. Some days it hardly seemed worth the effort.

"I guess I'm the type of guy who can't learn another language," I told myself. Or in another version: "This is stupid: I'm never going to learn this language."

Once doubt settles into the mind, removing it can be tough. This problem is common in the martial arts, especially for those who train at a high competitive level. Losing a competition, injuries, and getting your ass kicked daily in practice just to wake up and do it all over again are not for the timid.

But without a *why*, I couldn't apply what I knew from martial arts to language. I understood enough of the language to carry on small talk, order food, ask directions, and get around with day-to-day activities. My friends as well as the instructors both spoke English, so I could have gotten through my whole stay without having to learn the language for real.

But then my *why* found me.

Bem vindo ao Brasil (Part II)

I had been away from Brazil for only one month to renew my visa, but when I returned to Rio, the sweltering jungle heat had vanished. I welcomed the seasonal change as the southern hemisphere slipped into autumn. Not what most Americans think of as autumn—it was still hot—but a much more bearable eighty to eighty-five degrees during the day, much like October in Houston. Regardless of the weather, I had only one thing on my mind: training. But life had more in store for me.

While my tourist visa was only valid for three more months, I intended to stay much longer. A foreigner with a tourist visa is permitted to stay for only three months at a time and for no longer than six months within a year. At first, I was afraid to violate my visa's terms for fear of being deported and not allowed to return—or worse, being put in a Brazilian jail! But it turned out many of my teammates also had expired visas. One guy had even been living in Brazil for three consecutive years. I did some research and learned that you were fined only 25 reais per day past your visa's expiration date, with a maximum fine of 750 reais—about $300 US at the time. I initially stayed for three months, then returned home to see family and renew my visa for another three months. This time, I decided that I would stay for about eleven months more—illegally.

As crazy as it felt when I first arrived, returning to the bustling streets and chaos of Rio was like coming back home. I had missed the place. It's true that while I was away, my limited Portuguese had gotten a little rusty, and that's when I began thinking I should just give up on becoming fluent. Still, it was great to be back. I got settled in quickly, moved back in with Dennis, and hopped right back into training mode. Even with a couple of new faces at the dojo, it was like I had never left. I jumped right back into the joyful, sweat-filled days on the mat.

Meeting Fate

There's a little restaurant on the Brazilian island where I lived called Bar do Cícero—or simply "Cicero's Bar"—set on the canal that connects Ihla Primeira to Barra da Tijuaca. It has this great outdoor thatch-roofed patio that sits right on the water where boats tie up. There the air is alive with the bossa nova and the aromas of spicy grilled shrimp and beef. Many of the islanders come and just hang out, have parties, or mingle. Some days it was crazy busy, and other days it had only a few people. What I enjoyed most is that Cicero's had incredible, cheap food, which was why I frequented it several times per week.

Two months after arriving, I was hanging out at Cicero's with a friend from Australia, eating, enjoying the food and the view. I looked over my shoulder and saw this beautiful young woman—with silky, dirty blond hair halfway down her back and a proud, funny way of lifting her chin—sitting with her friends. I remember being taken by the inviting warmth of her deep brown eyes. In other words, this girl had it going on.

I've never been great at approaching women. Like a lot of guys, my shyness would sometimes take over—and that was with English-speaking girls. This very pretty woman glanced at me, gave a bashful smile, and turned away. Women in Brazil are typically a little more confidently and openly sensual than American women. They seem to be more comfortable in their own skin and with the power they have over men. Not her. She seemed just as shy as I was, if not more, but she did seem interested.

I was smitten, but not quite enough to get up and trip through my limited Portuguese. Approaching a woman is difficult enough without adding a language barrier to the mix. Still, as I continued to eat, I thought about ways to approach her.

Just a few minutes after I first saw her, Cicero came up and greeted me: "*Olá, gringo!*" That part I understood; Cicero always called me gringo. The next part I sort of got the gist of: "Come, I have a girl I want you to meet." I wasn't sure I trusted his judgment, and I didn't know who he was talking about, but he insisted. So I followed him, worrying that he was about to drop me off with some stranger I wasn't interested in and disappear.

But as we approached the woman he wanted me to meet, my heart raced a little faster. Cicero was leading me to *the* woman—the same woman who had shyly flirted with me. Now I was looking forward to the introduction: *This is fantastic—it's her!*

As he introduced me to Ingrid, she looked at Cicero as if she were mortified and embarrassed about what he was doing. But Ingrid later admitted, many months into our relationship, that she had put Cicero up to our introduction. She's as smart as she is beautiful—sensing that I might not have made a move, and knowing *she* wasn't going to ask, she convinced him to bridge the gap for us. I'm glad she did.

Everything Coming Together

Six months later, Ingrid and I were still dating. Ever since that day in Cicero's, we were nearly inseparable. I had never met a girl who fit my life so perfectly. Not that everything was perfect. We were still human and had fights and did the stupid things all couples do, but I felt like we belonged together.

It was now December, and summer was rolling back in with all its sultry fury. Other than making time for Ingrid, meeting her parents, and getting to know her better, everything continued as it had before: training, down time, more training. Oh, one thing changed: I no longer took the bus. Ingrid had informed me that people got robbed on buses all the time. I'd known about the dangers but was a little naïve. She'd shared stories about buses being held up, just like trains or stagecoaches in the American Wild West. We took taxis from that point forward—though sometimes, when she wasn't around, I still hopped on a bus.

Because of Ingrid, I finally had a reason to master Portuguese. I think I had more of a desire to master her language than she had to master mine. "I live in Brazil. Why would I want to learn English?" she said pragmatically. But whether it was part of my male drive or something else, I had finally found my *why* when it came to Portuguese. I was becoming more fluent but not as fluent as I'd hoped.

We were starting to get more serious by the time her birthday came around in late August. I wanted to get her something special, but I knew I couldn't get her anything expensive because I couldn't afford to spend too much. So I got a couple of flowers and chocolates and a birthday card. I decided to use my new Portuguese proficiency to write her something really romantic in the card. I thought, "I can write this and put some heart into it." I wanted to make sure I wrote it correctly, so I searched my *501 Portuguese Verbs* book, and I found the word *gozar*, which had the definition of "to really enjoy oneself." Perfect. To me, that word was far better than just *liking* someone. I wanted to show that I enjoyed my time with her.

On her birthday, I surprised her with the flowers, chocolate, and the card that had my handwritten inscription, which, in my mind, translated to, "I hope you enjoy this day as much as I enjoy every day being with you." Pretty sweet, right?

When I gave it to her, I must have had this smug, happy look on my face like *this is super romantic—I really did a good job.* I waited patiently for her to give me an *oh-how-sweet* expression and a big hug. Instead, her eyes just got big, she angled her head and stared at me with bewildered look and in Portuguese said, "Do you know what this means?"

My self-assuredness vanished. "Yes?" I sputtered.

You may know that the word *gay* in English used to mean happy, but now it refers to same-sex relationships. Well, it's kind of like that. *Gozar* used to mean *to enjoy oneself,* but these days it's slang for . . . um . . . orgasms.

She did her best to politely explain my faux pas. "It says, 'I hope you climax this day as I climax every day with you.'"

Great. Instead of being romantic, I sounded like a pig. It took me a few minutes to explain what I meant before she smiled. We were able to laugh about it later, but at the time, my embarrassment was at level ten!

On December 18, 2004, I attended the annual Gracie Barra barbecue, a year-end casual get-together for instructors and students. It was held on a small, walled estate in the Barra with beautiful greenery, a large lawn, and a swimming pool. The strange thing was having a full-blown summer party with the aroma of grilling meat, laughter from the pool, and everybody in their *sungas* (Speedos) only a week before Christmas. A White Christmas is never a Houston sort of thing, but neither are pool parties.

As the afternoon waned, Master Carlos Gracie Jr. (or Carlinhos, as he was commonly known), called everyone over to have a seat. Then he began awarding the new black belts. Some of the guys on the team had hinted that I was getting mine, but I didn't really believe them. I'd only been training for about seven years, and the average BJJ black belt takes close to around ten years. As Master Carlinhos read through the list, I happily applauded the names listed—people who had all become friends of mine over the past several months. The whole event felt surreal. We were all so laid back and casual. There was no pomp and circumstance, no belt test, no belts handed out. Just an announcement, a handshake, a short speech.

As Carlinhos neared the end of the list, my mind wandered a bit. But then he repeated himself, and my ears perked up. *What* had he said? My friends were patting my back, urging me to go up.

He had read my name. He couldn't have, but he did. I was getting my black belt in Brazil, the motherland of BJJ, and from the man who had helped spread the art around the world.

I didn't feel like I was ready. As with any significant life change, my excitement was matched only by my feeling of uncertainty. You might be prepared, well-studied, and eager, but you're never ready. There were black belts who were more accomplished, had a more intricate style, and had more advanced games than I did. The only thing I knew for sure was that I still didn't know everything about jiu-jitsu and had a lot more to learn. But who was I to argue with the leader of the top jiu-jitsu team in the world at that time?

As I walked to the front of the crowd, I was encouraged to give a short speech. And, of course, I needed to give this speech in Portuguese. I was almost unable to speak. Surrounded by all these great martial artists, sweating under the hot summer sun while trying to formulate my thoughts in a language I was just beginning to grasp—nervous is putting it mildly. And yet somehow I got through it pretty smoothly. I felt like Will Farrell during the debate scene in the movie *Old School* (great movie), when he answers a ridiculously tough question like he's channeling someone else.

What did I say? All I remember is that I thanked all of the people who made this possible: all my training partners, Alvis Solis, Carlos Machado, and Bill Lorenz, my parents as well as all of my new friends from Gracie Barra.

That was it. I was now a black belt. All the years of training, sweating and pouring myself into this passion had come to this moment—only I didn't have a belt yet. I had to buy that myself. I still remember feeling like a little kid the day I went to the "Vitamins and Minerals" shop at the Barra Shopping Mall to get it. I had gone to Brazil to further my training. I wasn't expecting to achieve my black belt while I was still there.

But that's not the only unexpected thing I brought back.

Welcome Back to Texas—and Reality

I thought training in Brazil, being away from my home and family, and living meagerly was tough. I had no idea that life would soon get even more difficult. Reading books had taught me to persist and ask, "What am I going to take from this?" When I focused on my own self-development, progress, and growth, there was no way I could fail, because every failure is only an event. It's an event I can learn from, so I how could I fail?

Before I left Brazil, Ingrid and I discussed our relationship. I was crazy about her, but I wasn't sure if this was *it*, whatever "it" is. We were young and didn't have enough life experience to know what was best for us under the circumstances. We had a decision to make, and I wasn't sure she felt as serious about our relationship as I did. It's funny how people avoid the tough conversations because we're afraid the answer won't be what we want it to be.

So we had the talk and I knew there were only two outcomes: either "This is it. It's been fun. Thanks for the laughs," or "We're going to make this work." I was relieved when it turned out we both wanted to keep our relationship going. Even if we didn't know where it would end, at that moment we were committed. To get a better understanding of what would be required for her to move back to Texas with me, we visited a local immigration attorney in downtown Rio.

The attorney was very friendly and started chatting about the possibilities. As we sat in his cramped office, he explained, "Well, you can either get married here, or you can get married in America. It really doesn't matter. It won't make the process any faster one way or the other."

Married? We were just dating, and I was only twenty-three. I asked if there were other visas she could apply for.

"Not really. She's not going there for a specific job, you said. She's not going to be attending school. The only option is a fiancée visa."

Ingrid and I were faced with reality: either we break up, or we get married. Super romantic, right? What we wanted was something equal to a dating visa or an I'm-really-into-you visa. But after doing some research, we discovered that she wouldn't even qualify for a tourist visa. At that time, the restrictions were very tight.

After leaving the lawyer's office, we had a lot to discuss. The attorney told us that, after she arrived, we would have ninety days to get married or the visa would expire. Based on that, we devised a plan. She would come to America, and we'd continue to date over the ninety-day period. Near the end, if we still wanted to live together in Texas, we would get married. We had made our decision.

And so four months after earning my black belt, in March 2005, I returned home to Texas. I hadn't intended to stay in Brazil as long as I had, but meeting Ingrid changed a lot of things. It was difficult to say goodbye, but I was ready to come home and start a new chapter in my life. Before Ingrid could join me, I had to return to Texas first, get settled in, and file the appropriate paperwork. I left Ingrid with the promise that she would eventually be allowed to join me in the US. I had no idea just how difficult it would be to make that happen.

My original goal had been to immerse myself in the language and culture of the martial art that had become my life. I had achieved that. Having the black belt and falling in love with Ingrid were just the icing on the proverbial cake. Now it was time to get to work—but first I had to get past customs in Rio. Remember, my tourist visa was good for a maximum three-month stay, and I had been there over a year. The fine I owed if caught was 750 reais, or $290, which I had in my pocket. In fact, that was about all that I had left.

As I wandered through the vast airport with its wide halls of cream-colored stone, I mentally practiced explaining in Portuguese that I knew I had stayed illegally and that I had the money for the fine. By the time I approached the security agent, who held a phone between his ear and shoulder, I was a sweaty bundle of raging nerves. But since he was on the phone, I held back on the speech for now and just handed him my passport.

Still talking animatedly on his phone, he grabbed it, gave it a quick glance, peeked at me, stamped it, and waved me on, returning his full attention to his call. I walked away with the money safe in my pocket, for which I was grateful. I needed every penny I could get to help start my business.

Back in Houston, I spent a couple of weeks getting situated at my dad's home, getting my affairs in order, and catching up with a few friends. Then it was time to get to work. My dad kept his promise to let me use the garage to teach jiu-jitsu. Honestly, I'm not sure I could have started it anywhere else, and even if I had started in a traditional studio space, it wouldn't have been mine. I'd have to get a loan, and then I'd be working on borrowed time. My dad's garage made sense from every angle.

After long days scrubbing, sweeping, mopping, and painting the garage until it said something more like "martial arts studio" than "mildewed, oil-stained Houston garage," I was ready to begin. I had a few old friends and former training partners show up for my first class. I was officially in business.

Now it was time to find an immigration attorney, and two weeks later, with the help of a friend of a friend, I did just that. This attorney confirmed what the Brazilian attorney had told us: a fiancée visa was our only option. I taught a bunch of private lessons to save up the $1,000 to pay him, and he showed me the necessary forms and walked me through the process.

Then things got interesting. Ingrid needed a sponsor, someone who could prove that she would be financially supported so she wouldn't end up on government assistance. That person couldn't be me because I hadn't been functionally employed for a couple of years and had sold almost everything I owned. With my brand-new handful of students, I hardly made enough to support myself, so I knew the application would be denied if I attempted to sponsor her. My parents also didn't financially qualify to help.

Bill came to the rescue yet again. I promised him he would never actually have to pay a cent for anything. I had no other recourse than to have a qualified sponsor sign for the application. He saved the day. When I submitted the application in August 2005, the attorney told me the process usually takes six months to complete, but he had a "good feeling" it might only take three to four. That meant we could be together before the end of winter. At least, that's what I thought it meant.

Persisting through Setbacks and Mistakes

Many people give up when the challenges of life become overwhelming. This is a shame, because they usually quit right before things get really interesting, just when they're on the verge of a major breakthrough.

In the midst of struggling to start a business, dealing with an intense physical setback (more on that later), and getting reestablished as a US citizen, I was eagerly awaiting the day when Ingrid could join me. Though I was essentially broke, we continued to call each other a few times a week, and I would fly down to visit when I could. Ingrid's uncle, who lived in the US, was a retired airline employee, so he was able to secure me free buddy passes . . . under one condition: I had to transport his merchandise for him. No, it wasn't drugs, weapons, or anything that Hollywood. His merchandise? Accordions. He had some sort of business buying accordions in the US and selling them back in Brazil. My job was to bring them down with me, to avoid duties or something like that. I never understood his business model, and though I probably should have, I never looked in the cases to make sure he wasn't hiding any other *merchandise* in the accordions. Occasionally customs would stop me to ask for taxes and duties, but Ingrid's uncle had supplied me with receipts from eBay showing they were under the legal limit. All that mattered was that Ingrid and I were able to see each other for the small price of being an accordion mule. And I don't mean the smuggling kind of mule—accordions are quite large!

As I got more students through old connections and word of mouth, three to four months quickly turned into six months. I started calling the attorney's office every other day, checking on the status of Ingrid's visa application. The young lady he had put in charge of our case was very nice, but there was nothing she could do. "The process is just taking a little longer than expected," she always said.

That was an understatement. I'd hoped to see Ingrid in three or four months; it turned into a total of fifteen. Yes, fifteen. I flew down to visit her four times during that period, each time staying for one to two weeks and lugging along two heavy accordions as my payment for the free ticket. They say absence makes the heart grow fonder, and I suppose that's true, but I found myself griping to our attorney's poor assistant, trying anything I could do to expedite the application. I suppose if it were only a time issue, perhaps it wouldn't have been such a big deal, but then I got news that rattled me and put a damper on my relationship with Ingrid.

Fifteen months after filing the application, we learned the good news: it was approved! Now all I had to do was send the sponsorship paperwork down for her to file with the US Consulate or something like that. It should have been easy.

I shipped the paperwork to her and got ready to see her within a week or so—but I screwed up. First, the Affidavit of Support was not notarized as it should have been, and second, I had placed my name where Bill's signature should have gone and vice versa. All by accident, because I was an *idiot*! Even if they let her reapply, there was a six-month waiting period to submit a second application, and second applications are rarely approved.

Ingrid had gotten mad at me before. Nothing topped this. She was so angry she refused to speak to me, and she had every right to be. It came down to me not paying attention. I had no excuses.

When the moment of realization set in, I panicked. I remember

thinking, *Crap, they might not let her in at all now!* After dating and longing to see each other, the thought that I made one mistake that could
cost me the best relationship I had ever had felt devastating. The mistake weighed heavily on my mind, and I felt sick over it.

But to my enormous relief, two long days later the National Visa
Center gave me a break. I was able to correct the error, correctly fill
out the paperwork, have it notarized, and send it off to Ingrid. She was
excited about her imminent visit, and so was I. Though her arrival was
delayed by another two weeks, I finally met her at Bush Intercontinental Airport in the second week of November 2006. When we she came
out of the terminal, she ran toward me, her gorgeous face glowing with
pleasure, and we embraced for the first time on US soil. It's a moment
etched in my mind.

Making Adjustments

It took some time for Ingrid to get used to living in the United States.
It was a culture shock even greater than my own experience adjusting
to Brazil. I at least had a community of BJJ students who welcomed me;
Ingrid only had me, and I was busy for most of the day. She spoke very
little English at the time, and we were living together in my dad's house
with my fledgling jiu-jitsu school, with little nearby for her to do. Back
then, the outskirts of Houston where we lived had little to offer besides
cow pastures, residential developments, and a shopping mall—quite a
switch from the constant bustle of the Barra. Plus, she didn't know anyone yet, so it was lonely for her in the beginning. I joked that at least
I knew Ingrid didn't love me for my money. In fact, this change was a
step down for her.

Within a month Ingrid got more acclimated to her new life here
with me, and our relationship grew past my thoughtless mistake that
almost ended her chance of becoming a citizen. After being separated
for so long, relying on phone calls and my four brief visits during that
fifteen-month span, I relished seeing her every day again. Seeing her
almost daily in Brazil was something I had taken for granted. We got
so used to the idea of being together, we almost forgot that we only had
ninety days to get married or she'd be forced to return home.

It was over two months into her stay when we woke up one morning and were like, "Oh, yeah—we need to get married or break up!" Possibly our previous hesitation came from our fear of commitment. But now our relationship had survived culture shock, separation, and major disappointment. When the time came to make the decision, for both of us the choice was clear. We had very little money between the two of us, so we arranged a courthouse wedding—just us, my father and mom, and her sister (a world traveler who was able to be in town for that day), and a justice of the peace. I didn't even have enough money for a proper engagement ring, so Ingrid ended up wearing a simple band, and I borrowed my father's wedding band. Eighty-three days after Ingrid arrived, we became husband and wife, with only seven days to spare. Many challenges faced us then—my health, my school, and bad investments—but for that one beautiful moment, all that mattered was her.

I had traveled to Brazil for an adventure and to further my martial arts training, with no idea what else life had in store for me. I left with a black belt and the love of my life. With my *whys* firmly in mind, I had persevered. It's easier if you have no other options because, for me, Brazilian Jiu-Jitsu was just about the only thing I wanted to do. On the other hand, I was ready to give up Portuguese until I had an excellent reason to learn it—a powerful *why*.

Just because I was now a black belt didn't mean my training was over. Martial arts are a lifelong study, with dedication to never-ending improvement—what the Japanese call *kaizen*. Besides, my struggles were not getting any easier. When I returned home, I faced more challenges and thieves than I had in Brazil. I had entered an arena called "business," and in that ring, I was a complete white belt.

Everything that happens to you is a form of instruction if you pay attention.

—Robert Greene[8]

Surmounting difficulty is the crucible that forms character.

—Tony Robbins[9]

CHAPTER 4

Discipline and Dedication

White Belt All Over Again

The difference between a dream and the life you desire is that one requires thought while the other requires relentless action in the face of failure. Dreaming might be the reason we begin, but by itself, it is meaningless without action. Some might say, "I'll take that course after summer," or "I'll start that business right after I 'know enough'" (whatever that means). I've learned that taking a step is more important than planning the step. Yeah, you can take a misstep—I've taken plenty of missteps in both business and life—but taking a misstep is better than never taking any step; at least you moved.

You don't have to have the *right* set of circumstances to get started with anything. I didn't know anything about business during the garage days. I don't think I knew what the word "entrepreneur" meant. My goal to teach was driven purely by a desire to continue doing what I love: teaching and training jiu-jitsu every day.

Learning about business was like being a white belt all over again. Actually, it might have been worse. At least as a new student in a dojo,

---

8 Robert Greene, *Mastery* (New York: Viking, 2012), 12.

9 Tony Robbins, *Awaken the Giant Within: How to Take Immediate Control of Your Mental, Emotional, Physical and Financial Destiny!* (New York: Simon & Schuster, 1991), 489.

you're guided by a set of principles and a code of conduct. Assuming you're in a good school, you know that, as you learn the basics, you're in a safe environment being led by experienced, ethical leaders. Business is more like a cage match with no holds barred and a few competitors who like to cheat; I jumped in with both feet.

I had just returned from Brazil, and after getting settled in, I began outlining my concept of a business plan and my teaching methodology: how I was going to structure my school's curriculum. The plan was laughable in hindsight, but I had to start somewhere. It's easy to get hung up on specifics and get overly detailed in the planning stage. Winston Churchill was spot on when he said, "Plans are of little importance, but planning is essential." What I think he meant is that planning forces you to consider various aspects of a situation. Planning teaches a person how to construct something with the available tools at hand. It all might go to crap once you start, but those experiences become tools for future use. Boy, did I get involved in some crap, but we'll get into that in a later chapter.

The first step in my plan was getting my dad's garage at least somewhat suitable to teach students. My dad's house sat on one acre all by itself, with a long driveway set back from the road. With plenty of room for students to park in the front yard and only one neighbor, there was little chance of anyone complaining about me operating a martial arts school in the neighborhood.

The garage itself was a two-car garage with two sections: a front section where the cars parked that measured twenty feet by twenty feet, and a back section accessible through an interior door that led to a small workshop area. It was a good-sized garage, but when I took it over, that front section was full of years of my dad's belongings. It took some serious effort to clear it out. It's amazing how much stuff we accumulate through life. Most of it was garbage. I mean, it was literally trash that had to be thrown out. The rest of it I crammed into the small workshop area in the back.

I spent a good part of the first week cleaning it out, working tirelessly to get the garage ready. At the end of one day, I felt a twinge in my back. A little pain went down my leg. Damn, it was back.

I'd felt that pain for the first time when I returned from Brazil after my initial three-month stay, back before I'd met Ingrid: a tingling pain trickling down my leg. Not intense pain, but enough to be annoyingly uncomfortable. I thought it could be something more, and I at least wanted to be rid of the annoying pain, so I had reached out to a chiropractor I knew. He gave me a very different answer. After a series of tests, pokes, prods, and an X-ray, he gave me a serious look.

"I think you have a bulging disc."

That didn't sound too good. Here I was ready to return to Brazil to continue my training, and he's telling me I should stay to get an MRI and, if it was serious, even consider back surgery. That sounded even worse. I'd watched my dad go through a double disc herniation surgery, and I didn't want to think about it. My priority was training. I'd decided to just deal with the little bouts of pain as they occurred, and I did fine for over a year back in Brazil.

So when the pain returned while cleaning out the garage, I ignored the tingle and continued preparing the garage for students.

Once the main garage was cleared, I was ready to open . . . almost. Next on my rudimentary business plan's to-do list was to locate some mats. Remember, Brazilian Jiu-Jitsu focuses on grappling and ground fighting, so concrete won't do.

A good friend of mine offered to lend me some interlocking puzzle-type mats. They were designed for more traditional martial arts, not grappling, but they were better than concrete for the short term. With the garage cleaned out and mats laid down, Team Tooke Martial Arts opened its doors—or the one big garage door, to be exact—in April 2005 with even less fanfare than when I was awarded my black belt. It felt good, but I didn't take time to congratulate myself. What's a school without students? It's just a cushioned garage. Now it was time to work.

The First Students

Up until this time, I had been following a dream without any sense of how I was going to get there. I didn't have any business education or detailed plans or anything except some books. Actually, in the early days of the school, I only had one book: *How to Open and Operate a Successful Martial Arts School*, by John Graden (a gift from Alvis Solis). While it might be antiquated by today's standards, what little I knew about the business side of running a martial arts school I'd learned from that book, so for me it was indispensable.

In some ways, I guess I was fortunate to have only one dream to focus on. Some people have two or three or a dozen things they'd like to do, and I was left with only one after the SEAL option vanished. My plan was simple. One, learn Brazilian Jiu-Jitsu as best I could by spending as much time on the mat as possible. Two, I would open a school and teach. My commitment to that vision is what kept me going.

If you only get one thing out of this book, I hope it's this: you must cultivate a sense or faith that life will ultimately work out in your favor. Whether it's opening a business, learning martial arts, or following any dream, focus on the outcome and take one step at a time into this new world you know nothing about. But you must balance that optimism with reality, lest you become a victim of delusion. Confront the reality of your circumstance with brutal honesty, then get to work. All you may know in the beginning is the basic direction in which you would like to go. You don't have to know how you're going to do it, only that you are. Don't get attached to the *how*. Focus on your *why*—the direction you want to go—and don't get deterred when things don't go your way, because they won't.

Learning as you go is both terrifying and exhilarating at the same time. Looking back, I had no permits to open a school in that garage. I'm not even sure if it was allowed under zoning ordinances. Let's not bring up insurance, either. I didn't have any. I'm not recommending anyone to follow my path, but what I am saying is that sometimes you have to act more than think.

Despite my lack of know-how, my first few students filed through the door. The first was my cousin, Andrew Craig, who was fresh out of high school. Another was Jeremy Trahan, whom I've known since we were eighteen and training together at Alvis's school, as well as Jace Pitre, among a handful of other old friends. Will and Brandon Lorenz, Bill Lorenz's sons, popped in sporadically, but they were so busy with wrestling, school, and other sports that I didn't see them as often.

Another student was Tom Dinklage, a former teammate of mine. I had trained with him when I was nineteen, back when we were both students at Solis Martial Arts. He was a purple belt in jiu-jitsu and owned his own academy, Precision Martial Arts. After I returned to Texas, he called me and said, "Hey, I'd like to train with you." I was happy to have him.

With the arrival of the first few students, I went about making my first mistake: the schedule. I thought I could offer an open schedule. I started with two slots: eleven in the morning until one o'clock, and then another slot in the evening from seven to nine. I know now that two-hour classes are too long unless you're preparing for competition or focusing on a specialty. Tom was able to take advantage of the first class and was there nearly every weekday. Most days it would just be the two of us. He got daily private classes, and I got to continue my training with a motivated and hardworking student. It wasn't so great for my business, but I really enjoyed training with him nonetheless.

Those were humble beginnings, with only a handful of students. I'd get up, make sure I had a cooler of ice-cold water ready for my students— that was my major daily to-do. Some days I'd just hang around an empty garage, waiting.

About two weeks after opening, my dad's friend Myron, a fellow martial artist, offered me a real wrestling mat suitable for groundwork and takedowns. It measured twenty feet square, the exact size of the garage. The mat was a godsend. Though it was well-used and smelled a little funky, it worked perfectly.

Despite the new mat, working out of the garage wasn't ideal. By that time my dad was semi-retired and was home most days. Students who came to train would park, go into the messy house, say *hi* to my dad, and change in the cramped bathroom. It was okay for those who already knew me and my dad, but it did get a little awkward with new students. I didn't let that stop me, though occasionally my bulging disc would remind me that it hadn't gone away.

Marketing 101

A few months had passed, and I was progressing at a snail's pace. Clearly I needed to grow my business. I had a small group of students who came consistently. I had a monthly revenue target in mind for what I needed in order to move out of the garage and into a new studio. If I was ever going to make that move possible, I knew things had to change. Marketing was the answer, but like everything else in business, I was clueless about how to do it. Most marketing is expensive, though I suppose everything seems expensive when you have no money. I needed to find a cheap way to get the word out.

Fortunately, I found gold in my dad's garage. Not literal gold, though that would've been nice. While cleaning, I found a bunch of quarter-inch-thick plywood pieces left over from his construction projects, each about the size of a piece of paper. I painted them white, bought some nice italicized stencils, and made signs in black letters that said "Brazilian Jiu-Jitsu" and listed my cell phone number. Others read "Free Class" or "Free Week." Then I went around the area nailing them to telephone poles (yes, I knew this was illegal), and my dad helped me build a big sign for the front yard. Then I sat back waiting for the phone to ring.

It didn't.

In 2005, jiu-jitsu was really starting to make its way into the mainstream with the huge growth of the UFC. But it was still relatively unknown as a martial art. The general public knew about karate and kung fu and tae kwon do. But jiu-jitsu? What the hell is that? I laugh at my ignorance now, but I just did whatever I thought might work. In fact, it never occurred to me that it might *not* work—that my whole plan might fall apart. Instead, by taking small steps, I got the sense that *Wow, this is actually happening.* I had a school. I had some so-called marketing. The excitement I felt by doing something scary and different was enough to keep me going even if the results were not there yet.

It would have been easy to stop and think of why my school might fail. I could have reasoned that nobody's going to want to train in somebody's unair-conditioned garage in Houston in the middle of summer. I could have dwelled on all the other reasons it might not work. Instead, I was thinking, "If I do make calls, put up the signs, and try other tactics, I will probably get at least a couple of students. That will give me X amount of income, and then I will be able to save some."

So I kept going. It's all I knew how to do: keep going. One thing I've learned in my life is when you commit to something, see it through at least long enough to have truly learned something of value. If you feel passionate about what you're doing, or are drawn to it, you must keep going no matter what happens.

But then I suffered a setback that cast doubt and uncertainty into my life like never before.

Pain in My Backside

About three months into my business venture in the garage, my back pain went from uncomfortable to unbearable in a matter of twenty-four hours. It was the summer by then, and I remember this particular day was especially hot, even for Houston. Yves Edwards and Josh Thomson, two UFC fighters, were in town training together. Yves and I had become good friends over the years, and I jumped at the chance to train with them. I had a blast. (Over the years, I have had the opportunity to be in Yves's corner for numerous UFC fights as his jiu-jitsu coach. I consider him one of my best friends.) Other than training with world-class athletes and the heat, the day seemed like any other.

I didn't notice it during training, but driving to visit my mom afterward I began feeling a sensation like somebody was cramming a baseball into my spine. I ended up staying at her house that night. She offered me the couch to sleep on, and that was fine. I'd slept on that couch before.

But the couch was a mistake. Between each of the three firm seat cushions was a gap that offered zero support where I needed it most. Those gaps probably forced my spine to bend in the worst way. When I awoke the next morning, I was wrecked. Pain blistered through my back and down my right leg as if I were being impaled by a thousand needles, and I was unable to walk.

For the next hour or so, I tried to warm up my back with some gentle moves. Eventually I could function a little, take somewhat normal steps, and almost stand upright. This went on for weeks. It was incredibly painful to teach, but I had no choice. I needed to survive, and though the income from my teaching was meager, it covered my basic expenses. A few months back I had applied for Ingrid's visa and wanted to be able to support her when she arrived.

Over the next few weeks, I learned to adapt my movements while teaching class to avoid certain positions. Simple things like taking a drink from a water fountain became major accomplishments. Most people bend forward at the waist to take a sip, but not me. People must have thought I was psychotic—a young, healthy, fit guy at the water fountain sucking in the stream while doing an exaggerated side lunge.

Having the ability to move didn't mean I was pain-free—not by a long shot. I was coping with my intense discomfort by moving in different ways and wearing a back brace that was tight, itchy, and incredibly uncomfortable. Still, it kept everything from shifting around too much so I could train. I thought that maybe if I rested, stretched, and took well beyond the recommended dose of ibuprofen, eventually I'd be back to my old self, but it didn't happen.

After a couple of weeks of this, I began thinking I might never be the same ever again. I wasn't sure exactly what was wrong. Although I suspected it was the disc issue, I never had it diagnosed properly. I wasn't feeling depressed; it was more like a despondent, gloomy sense that my spine might never be the same, that a part of me was gone forever. I'd dedicated almost eight years of my life to one end, and now the realization that my career might be over weighed heavily on me, as did the thought of never competing again. I was only twenty-four, and I remember wondering if I were just going to be this *old-man* version of myself forever. I had watched my dad suffer from back pain for most of his life, and I began sensing that I was destined to endure this kind of pain forever.

I skipped competing at the world championships that year due to the injury. As a result, I missed my friend and current (as of this writing) Bellator World Champion, Rafael Lovato Jr., make history by becoming only the second non-Brazilian to win the world championships as a black belt. When I read this news online, I was blown away. Rafael is one of the greats of jiu-jitsu. He is the most decorated and successful American in the history of the sport. Still, that moment was bittersweet for me as I sat at home, sidelined from taking part myself. I felt a strange blend of pride and pity at the same time.

I've never let what I can't do determine my path. But obviously there were things I could no longer do because of the pain, and my self-administered health plan wasn't working. It was time to get help.

Of the many luxuries I did without in the early days, health insurance was one. My team of friends came through yet again. Vinnie, a good friend of mine, had a brother who was a radiologist, and he suggested an MRI scan—it was the best way to see what was happening in my spine. My mouth went dry when I heard price tag: $1,000. I had no idea how I was going to come up with that kind of money. But then, thankfully, he added that he'd do it for free. Vinnie, coincidentally, needed an MRI for his hurting shoulder, so his big-hearted brother offered to give each of us an MRI free of charge. If you've ever been in an MRI, you know how frighteningly intimidating the machine can be. Lying on a sliding table, I was shoved into a coffin-like hole so small I was afraid to breathe. Then the noise started. I'm fine with unpleasant noise, but these sounds were terrifying. It made this racket like somebody had mounted a series of air horns on a firetruck. Sometimes it was the horns, other times it was the sirens, and they were awful all the time. Then they would pause briefly, only to start again with zero warning. Again, if you've ever been inside an MRI machine, you know exactly what I'm talking about. Even with earplugs, this thing is loud!

Finally, the exam was over. The assistant gently rolled me out of the machine. As I began to sit up, the radiologist walked in through the door. With a smile on his face indicating that he had goods news, he said, "I've got some bad news for you." I got dressed and waited to hear my fate. I went into his office where he proceeded to "inform" me about how bad my diagnosis really was. "You see that?" he said, pointing to the image of my spine. "That's a normal disc. Now, see that disc—that big nasty black blob sticking into your spinal cord? That's the bad one." He still had his caring yet sadistic smile intact.

"So . . . how bad is it?" I asked, not really knowing how bad it was based on the image.

"That's one of the worst ruptures I've ever seen! We usually measure disc herniations in millimeters. You've got over a full centimeter!"

My bulging disc had ruptured (or *herniated*, as they say in medical circles). A rupture means that instead of acting like a cushion between my vertebrae like it's supposed to, my disc was oozing out of its place and putting pressure on my spinal cord. In the image, it looked like somebody had taken a sledgehammer to a jelly donut. A protrusion of half a centimeter is considered bad. My disc protruded over a full centimeter. With my health and career hanging in the balance, I considered my options.

Then I heard him say the dreaded *s* word: surgery.

Surgery? I had no insurance or money. I needed to cure my ailing back. Back home, I researched my options. If you've ever researched a diagnosis, you know that it can fill your mind with terrible thoughts. I've read stories about hypochondriacal medical students who develop the symptoms of the maladies they're studying. They even have a term called *intern's syndrome*. That's what I did after I began reading up on my prognosis and options. I read that a herniated disc in the lumbar region can lead to loss of erectile function or bowel control. Of course, my mind imagined the worst possible scenario: I'd lose both. Being young, wearing a diaper, and having no love life was not an option—though I suppose that if I had lost only bowel control, that would have put a damper on my love life all on its own.

My research did turn up some good news: sometimes surgery wasn't necessary. But I didn't know enough to make that call. My dad had had two herniated discs from working in construction his entire life. Eventually, surgery was his only option as he was unable to function and was the primary bread winner of our family.

Before I could meet with surgeons, I needed some health insurance to help with the expense. Insurance companies at that time could deny coverage for preexisting conditions. I may have *forgotten* to list my herniated disc on my insurance application.

With the insurance in place, and almost immediately after the thirty-day grace period, I visited with the first surgeon, a young guy who gravely contemplated the MRI images. There was no doubt in his mind, surgery was the answer. Not to me it wasn't. My research revealed that the long-term effects of surgery weren't sunshine and rainbows. The odds of being pain-free weren't great one way or the other. Looking down the road, the five-years-after-surgery versus five-years-without-surgery prognoses were almost identical in a majority of cases. A brief reprieve from the pain was hardly worth the trouble, in my mind. I thanked the surgeon and told him I was getting a second opinion, which I did: except the second surgeon agreed with the first. Ugh. My certainty about a nonsurgical solution eroded a little, but I still believed it was possible.

What scared me the most was the thought of my dad. I was just a boy at the time, maybe nine or ten, when he needed surgery for two herniated discs in his lower lumbar spine, and I remember him lying in bed in agony. He'd moan, and it terrified me. I was heartbroken to see him like that. He'd always been this intimidating, strong guy, and there he lay, unable to move to get more comfortable, screaming that it felt like his legs were on fire. There was nothing I could do for him. I didn't want to be in that same hell.

Fearful of receiving the same recommendation, I saw a third surgeon anyway. At this time, I had started to concede and lean toward the surgery option. My pain had peaked and was holding steady. I was tired of taking anti-inflammatories and seeing the chiropractor twice a week just for him to tell me, "You're coming along just fine. See you next week." Turns out, this third surgeon was a judo black belt, a style with many similarities to BJJ, and he also had a disc herniation like mine. After reviewing my records and the MRI image, he turned to me with a look of sympathy. I prepared myself for his recommendation for surgery, and I was ready to get that process started. If the adage that the third time's the charm is truth, then here was proof.

"Look," he said, "you don't have any nerve damage. All you have is pain."

"Well, it's not just pain," I said. "Some nights I can't sleep, I can't lean forward, I can't sit for more than five minutes without my back killing me . . . this has completely changed my life."

"True, but your nerves are still working fine. Sure, I could cut the disc out, but you'd still likely have the pain, and your spine would be even less normal than it is now."

We then discussed the options. Surgery was out for sure in my mind, especially with him confirming that I didn't have any of the nerve damage that could lead to limp-diaper-man syndrome or cause my leg to atrophy like my dad's did. He basically told me to rehab the crap out of my back, get strong and flexible, and that would allow me to be fairly normal. That's what he had done for his own herniation and was able to avoid surgery.

For the next few weeks, I managed the pain the best I could as I tried to scrape together the funds to get the rehab I so desperately needed. It was difficult to function, to be there for my fledgling school and my students. During this time, I made a trip to Brazil to see Ingrid, lugging those damned accordions, which would have been aggravating enough with a healthy back.

My support network came through again. The next time I spoke with Yves Edwards, I mentioned my trials since that day.

Unbeknownst to me, Yves would soon provide the glimmer of hope I needed.

A Snake, a Rat, and a Creepy Guy in His Underwear: Welcome to Team Tooke

Fluctuating as I was between extreme discomfort and seething pain, I began feeling a little dejected. It was never full-blown depression, but at times I felt like life as I'd known it—as I hoped it would be—was over. It seemed like it was taking forever for Ingrid to join me in Texas; my back was destroyed; and most days, my school had only one student. Though I didn't consider giving up on having a school, the thought certainly crossed my mind. Then I met Dr. Luu.

Dr. Minh Luu called me out of the blue one day. He was a friend of Yves Edwards and had trained briefly in jiu-jitsu, though not with me. He introduced himself and stated that he would like to come by and do some jiu-jitsu training. He came to the garage one evening for the first time. After class ended, we hung out and chatted. "Yves told me that you got a bit of a back problem?" he said.

"Yeah, you could say that," I replied half-heartedly.

We continued to chat. Turns out, he was one of the top sports rehab doctors in the area and worked with some of the top athletes in the country. So we came to a gentlemen's agreement. He would train at my academy, and in exchange, I would go to see him a couple of times per week to strengthen and rehabilitate my lower back.

This simple encounter was a turning point in my physical and, more importantly, mental and emotional well-being. Even with insurance in place, my co-payments on physical therapy were more than I could manage. At the time, my teaching rates were ridiculously low at $70 a month. Dr. Luu knew it wasn't a fair trade for his services, but he really wanted to help me.

Agreeing to train a student is one thing, but actually meeting and getting started can be something different. I remember the day Dr. Luu arrived for his first lesson. He showed up in his new, shiny truck in the middle of a typically hot summer's day. By this time, my dad had helped me enclose the front of the garage and installed a through-the-wall air conditioner. This did not mean the school was now cool—quite the contrary. The air conditioner was poorly matched against the immense space of the garage and all the heat pouring through gaps in the door. All it managed to provide was a brief respite of relief for the students who jogged past it during warmups.

Dressed in his typical work outfit, khakis and a button-down shirt, he looked at the garage and the house as he stood in the driveway, baking in the sun. "Um, where do I change?" he asked, holding up a gym bag.

This was always the weird part. I'm eternally grateful to my dad for helping me get started in my business. I might have been able to do it without him, but it would have been much harder. That being said, it was odd having to tell students where to change: the bathroom inside the house. Up until now, most of my students knew me, but here was a finely dressed doctor, a stranger, and I had to explain the delicate situation he was about to enter.

"Go through that door," I explained, gesturing toward the home. "The house is a bit messy. Ignore the snake and rat in the kitchen and my dad, who may or may not be in his underwear and will probably be watching the TV or feeding the snake—or both. The bathroom is then down the hallway to the left."

In a way I guess it was a modern *Kung Fu*–type rite of passage. If the underwear guy, the messy house, the snake (an eight-foot-long reticulated python my dad had inherited from a friend), and the rat, which was the snake's dinner, don't creep you out—then I will teach you. Dr. Luu was probably wondering what he had gotten himself into as he entered that house, but he passed the "test" and stuck around.

The arrangement couldn't have been any better. I was finally getting the help my back desperately needed, and Dr. Luu was getting training in a martial art he's since learned to love as much as I do. We are still great friends to this day.

Turning Points

The therapy, stretches, and adjustments made me almost human again. But I was still struggling to keep my business going. Students would come and go—that is, the few of them who even found out about the school. Despite the setbacks and my struggles learning to function again, the school crawled along.

Doubts plagued me. At this point, I was still wondering if my back would ever be at 100 percent again, and Ingrid was still stuck in Brazil waiting patiently for her visa to come through. Meanwhile I was trying to learn what I could about running a business. Unlike Brazilian Jiu-Jitsu, I had few teammates and no mentors. All I had were my few books and some inkling of a guess about what I was supposed to be doing.

In the beginning, everything I thought would help to grow the business didn't work at all. I could have thought, *Oh well. This didn't work, and I really thought it was going to. It must not be in the cards.* I learned that when I got attached to *how* it was going to happen, I'd get frustrated quickly. I learned to trust the process, focus on the next steps, and make adjustments where needed. Some people ask why I didn't get a job and teach part time as the school grew. That's a good question and, in hindsight, may have actually been a better decision. But mentally I didn't want to put myself there. I didn't want to straddle the fence. If I gave myself the out of getting a job—if I gave myself that source of security— I might never have succeeded.

I've met many who think that some people just have *it*, whatever *it* is. The right upbringing, education, innate talent, looks, brains, athletic ability. While it's true that some come from a strong sports background or have body types that are ideal for jiu-jitsu, because they have good musculature or skeletal structure, those alone will only take you so far. Natural disposition and other past training might help you advance through the first two belts quickly, but then you'll stall. At some point, the only thing that matters is quality time on the mat. It's the effort, showing up, pushing through, and never quitting that creates success in BJJ or any venture. You have to put in the work or "mat time." Degrees may help, body type might be good, but nothing—and I mean *nothing*— is a substitute for consistent, hard work.

After I opened the school, it seemed like one adversity after another. At least I was scraping together some money and my back was improving. Things were beginning to look up. The weather began cooling down and the days were getting shorter. Christmas approached—my first without Ingrid since meeting her—and I began to get into a groove, a routine, that made me feel like maybe I was getting on the right track. My persistence in business began paying off but only just a little.

I'm a little pessimistic, so I can understand why some people get nervous when things start going well. Just when I started coming into my own, my dad gave me the news.

"Travis, I've been meaning to tell you. I'm selling the house. You're going to have to move the school."

*Don't expect to be motivated every day to get out
there and make things happen. You won't be. Don't
count on motivation. Count on Discipline.*

—Jocko Willink[10]

*You must understand the following: In order to
master a field, you must love the subject and feel
a profound connection to it. Your interest must
transcend the field itself and border on the religious.*

—Robert Greene[11]

CHAPTER 5

Motivation and Mastery

When my dad told me that he was selling the house, mentally I understood. He was semi-retired and getting older, the large property was
getting to be too much to take care of, and he had a pretty good offer
from some investors. But my stomach dropped, and my thoughts raced
around a more self-centered idea: *What about my school?* Worry slithered
into my mind, and once it wrapped itself in knots, it refused to leave.

The school had been operating for about ten months, and now I was
being evicted . . . by my *dad*! Well, sort of. But if I were in his situation,
I would've sold, too. He had originally paid $80,000 for the home and
now, twelve years later, he was offered $230,000. This was enough to
pay off his mortgage, buy a small home in cash, and have a little in the
bank. It was a no-brainer to me. But I had to scramble to find a new
home for my school. How I was going to *pay* for the new location was
another matter entirely.

It was time for this bird to leave the safety of the nest, whether I wanted

---

10 Jocko Willink, *Discipline Equals Freedom: Field Manual* (New York: St. Martin's Press,
    2017), 68.
11 Robert Greene, *Mastery*, 31.

to or not. I now believe that this was a blessing—a catalyst that facili-
tated my future growth. The garage was enough to get by on. Without
this push, I might not have ever taken this next step. Being forced to
take that step forced me to grow. I think that it's in moments like this
where we experience the most growth—when we have to find a way to
make it work or quit.

When I share this story and other stories about change or loss, sometimes I'm asked how I stayed motivated. Motivation's got little to do with it.

Knowledge Is Good—Action Is Better

No matter how strong your *why*—your purpose—is, life still has its inevitable low points. I've had many: my parent's divorce, waiting for Ingrid's visa, suffering with my herniated disc, and having to relocate my
school when I didn't know how I was going to afford it, among others.
Not to mention the existential woes of just being human. Reconnecting
to your purpose is great, but sometimes you need something more.

For me, books have been as essential to my success—to getting me *un-
stuck*—as my mentors have been to my training. Back when I was nineteen, Jeremy Trahan, a friend I made at Alvis's school, introduced me to
some of Tony Robbins's tapes. Prior to that, I had a somewhat limited
view of my future options. My perspective on life completely changed
when I started reading the right self-help and personal development
books. A new world of possibilities opened up to me. For the first time
in my life, I believed that I could be exactly who I wanted to be, and
I was able to visualize what that looked like.

The knowledge I gained from books and personal development aid-
ed me during times of change. But knowledge can only take you so far.
Real growth comes from taking action on that knowledge. Tempting as
it is to read an entire book and enjoy the burst of motivation at the end,
I've learned to stop for a while when I get that Eureka! moment. If I read
about a way to reinforce a good habit, I stop reading and set up a plan
to implement that reinforcement before I read any further. Knowledge
isn't worth anything until it is put to use.

When I learned about the sale of my dad's home, I had to stop myself
from focusing on the loss. I'd learned that challenges are opportunities
in disguise—opportunities for me to grow. Here was my chance to apply

what I'd learned, to test that theory and focus on the opportunity instead of what I was losing. I certainly would have grown too comfortable if I'd been allowed to remain there. Sometimes situations force you out of your comfort zone, and that's when growth finally happens. So I hopped on the phone and reached out to my network. I cannot stress enough the importance of maintaining good relationships on your journey.

After a number of calls, I found the opportunity I was looking for. Steve Sanford, my friend and judo instructor, was the owner of several warehouse buildings that he would lease. He had twelve hundred unused square feet that he was willing to lease to me on a month-to-month basis for only $1,000 a month. That's unheard of in commercial rentals. Typically, there's a deposit of first and last month's rent plus security fees, and then you sign on for a minimum of a five-year lease. But Steve was *old school*. And I needed a *new school*. I had taught jiu-jitsu methods and concepts to his team and students on several occasions. Because of this, we had maintained a good working relationship over time. If we had not had this relationship, I'm pretty sure I would not have had this incredible opportunity.

Moving Day

I still can picture the day I got the keys to the new facility. This was really happening! I felt like a kid. That is, I felt somewhere between a kid with his first car and a kid at his first middle-school dance: excited and nauseous. I unlocked the door, stepped over the threshold, and traced every detail with my eyes. The studio's lighting was a little too dim; the beams had some cobwebs; the walls were scuffed up; and the air carried a dank, fetid odor like a locker room after a football game. But it was mine. Unlike the cramped quarters of the garage, it was a nice, open space with a small walled-off office in one corner and one bathroom with no shower. The only amenities the garage offered that this studio lacked: snakes and dads in their underwear watching TV. Nobody missed them.

But the joy of having a new home for my school was clouded by a lingering sense of dread: I was only making around $1,000 a month at the time, with about fourteen or fifteen students. I had enough to pay the rent, but not quite enough to pay the utilities—and forget about any extras. You talk about stress—I was freaking out. It's one thing to focus on the goal, but it's another thing to quiet those voices of doubt that creep in and whisper to the darkest, most self-destructive area of your brain—the parts that like to imagine the worst possible scenarios.

Private lessons were essential in helping me stay financially solvent at that time. When I'd get a request for a private lesson, I remember acting all professional and saying, "Sure, let's look at the calendar and set the appointment." But on the inside I was psyched that I got to pay the electric bill that month! Through word of mouth, and with the rise in popularity of BJJ in the martial arts community, other schools began contacting me to conduct seminars. That helped to pay the bills, too.

Speaking of money, grappling mats were once again in short supply. The old ones from the garage were not big enough to fill the space of the new building. Fortunately Steve, my new landlord, loaned some tatamis (traditional Japanese mats) he was no longer using. They were good enough with only one minor issue: the corners curled up so the mats were a little bowl-shaped. When the students jogged around the studio, I had to remind them to be careful so they wouldn't trip and break their legs.

Although the school had moved to its new place, I was still living with my dad in his new place. Things were crazy for a while. I am forever grateful for my dad and all the help he has given me along the way. That said, like with many father-son relationships, we argued, butted heads, and downright didn't get along much of the time. Being a twenty-four-year-old dependent with no money wasn't exactly a motivating factor in my life at this time. A home move is hectic enough, but a little more so with my dad. As I've said before, my dad has an affinity for collecting odds and ends, and it's amazing how much clutter we amass when we're in living in one spot for years. He had bought a little ranch home in a subdivision, and my brother and I helped lug everything there. But beyond moving dad and my stuff, I also had to move a business. It's funny how, when things absolutely have to get done, we always find a way to do them. We moved my dad into his new house in the beginning of 2006, right around the same time my new location opened. It was tough, but we got it done.

Living with my dad helped me keep my expenses low. With just enough revenue to cover the school's expenses, I had little left for housing. But if my dad's new home hadn't had space, I know I would've found another way. I had made up my mind: I had to make teaching BJJ work somehow, whatever it took.

By nature, I'm not optimistic. When I was younger, my pessimism would often overwhelm me, and I would opt out of trying to reach certain goals or participate in different areas of interest. I now understand where these emotions come from and have learned to overcome them. Today when I experience those negative thoughts, I have a conversation with myself so that I can fully understand why it is happening. Then eventually I will say, "Are you done feeling sorry for yourself? Because nobody actually gives a shit and nobody's going to come fix this problem for you. It's time for you to get to work resolving this problem yourself." After saying that, it triggers me to leave that negative thinking and get back to work. If I hadn't developed this habit of snapping myself out of pessimism, it would have been easy for me to slip into a long-term pity party.

New student enrollments remained low even after opening in the new location. I still had the signs up around the area. But with that and some referrals, I was maintaining only the same number of students between drop-outs and new enrollments. The work to increase my financial situation had to start with my thinking. At that time, I had thought about my school like it was a Walmart: If I'm the cheapest around, I'll have more students. That thinking was wrong. By leaving that old garage and moving to a nicer place—a place where students would want to come—I was able to provide a better experience in a nicer facility and charge a higher tuition. In addition to that, my ability to lead productive and inspiring classes had improved over this time.

But a slightly higher tuition wasn't enough. Sure, now that I had commercial space, achieving my dream seemed more real to me than it was in the garage. I had leased a piece of real estate with a sign and everything. But I still needed to find more students, or this would be a short-lived dream. Nothing turns up the volume on those negative voices like a dwindling checking account.

Mastery of Anything Takes Work

With the new location opened, I felt more like a real businessman. But I still didn't know half of what I know now. Only twenty-five years old, I still had a lot to learn. With a more attractive location, I was able to secure a few more students, but still far fewer than I had hoped. I wanted to fast-forward to the part where the school was thriving, we were producing high-level black belts, and my finances were stable and growing.

I love how in movies like *Batman Begins* the filmmakers skim over the hard work with an inspirational montage to the beat of a rocking soundtrack. They're fun to watch, but I don't think I have to tell you that they're not real life. In real life, those two-minute-long montages take years or decades of consistent, disciplined, and often boring action. Day after day, week after week. Sometimes you have a soundtrack of your choosing—especially during workouts. Other times you're trying to drown out those doubts in your head that are trying to steal your energy and drive.

If you have goals to achieve, you must be willing to commit to daily effort to achieve them. Climbing mountains is great, but mountain climbers still put one foot in front of the other like the rest of us. In BJJ, the daily hours of training are infinitely more valuable than a new belt or a title. The belt or title is just a manifestation of the work coming together. You don't have complete control over exactly when you get your belt or an important win in a tournament, but you can control your decision to put in the daily effort. Consistently working on a goal is like compound interest: it's one of the most powerful forces that you can apply to your jiu-jitsu or anything else you're working toward. Yes, I had help along the way—every person who achieves their goal gets help—but I had to show up and put the work in whether I felt like it or not. That was true for achieving black belt and just as true for running a business. Regardless of your circumstances, you must keep doing the work. Inexplicable waves of depression and motivation are going to be a part of your journey. But keep doing the work. The fruits of your labor will show themselves in time.

By the time the school moved into the new building, I had begun to see the proverbial light at the end of the tunnel. Though I was sleeping on a twin mattress on the floor of a small bedroom in my dad's new house, still dealing with back pain and the physical therapy to make me whole again, and awaiting Ingrid's visa, at least I finally had a school with a little office that held a cheap chair and a basic little desk. But I still needed to learn, grow, and evolve as a person and a business owner.

Achieving mastery in jiu-jitsu requires the same investment as does achieving mastery in any of life's disciplines. I've said it before: time on the mat. I intrinsically understood that the more time I'd spend on the mat with my teammates, coaches, and professors, the better I'd get. It was no different for business.

But the road to mastery takes more than mat time alone. Mastery requires the four forces of motivation, purpose, passion, and discipline. They work together like the components of a fire. Let's look at how these forces work.

Remember my first encounter with BJJ—in my friend's house watching fights on VHS? I didn't say, "I don't know what this is, but this is my mission: to learn this art and teach it to others!" Nobody finds their way to mastery like that. For most, it starts with an interest. That's what it was for me, just an interest. I didn't know what Royce Gracie was doing in that fight, but it sure looked kind of cool.

And even after I got into BJJ, started learning the basics, I wasn't exactly on fire. If you remember, I took a break after winning in that first tournament at Alvis's school because I didn't think it was cool anymore. Interest will get you to try something. But with interest alone, you'll eventually falter. Interest is nothing more than an unlit match. It has potential, but by itself it's pretty useless.

That's why you need a spark of motivation. "Motivated" is often used to mean feeling pumped-up, excited, or inspired: *get motivated!* While these feelings do happen, and they feel great when they do, motivation, like interest, is only temporary. Motivation is like a lit match: bright and hot but quick to die. A lit match gives you enough light to see your immediate surroundings. It can start a fire or relight one that has gone out. When you feel like taking a break from the hard work or hanging it up (quitting), motivation can inspire you short term to keep it up.

This motivation is good. It can lead to a life change. But if you don't apply the lit match of motivation to something that can sustain your fire, it will go out. Apply it to some paper and kindling, though, and now you're getting somewhere.

Maybe some real-world examples would help.

If you're like a lot of people, you have a desire to improve your health. This could include specific goals such as losing fat, gaining muscle, eating healthier, increasing your aerobic capacity—or a combination of all these things. Maybe you then watch a YouTube video by some health guru with so much energy it's contagious. You now feel inspired and motivated to take action. You sign up for a gym, throw out all your Twinkies and chips, and post a goal on Facebook if you're feeling so bold.

But if all you've got is motivation, on that first morning you are supposed to work out, the fact that you didn't get enough sleep is enough resistance for you to stop—it just blows the match out.

Maybe that's because you motivated yourself with a weak word like *should*, as in *I should lose weight* (go to the gym, eat less, etc.). A *should* is nothing more than a wish. When's the last time one of your wishes came true when all you did was wish for it? Exactly.

So you need something more than that "should." You need a purpose.

A sense of greater purpose—your *why*—is the reason you need the fire. If your reason for your fire is to have something cool to look at while drinking beers with your buddies, it's a reason but not a strong reason. Some wet wood or a lighter that won't light is enough to put the kibosh on the idea and resign to sitting in the dark. But if you're about to die of exposure in the wilderness, your *reason* to follow through and get a fire going is more intense—wet wood or not.

Instead of a *should*, you find some deeper meaning in pursuing good health. A loved one died young because he didn't take care of himself; you want to be able to dance at your daughter's wedding; or you're sick and tired of feeling sick and tired all the time. Whatever this purpose is, this *why* has to be significant to you like survival in the wilderness.

To develop mastery, you have to search yourself and decide what you want beyond the "coolness" of achieving that thing you desire, what you want beyond the initial infatuation. For me, my purpose was connected with my joy in learning new things and improving, along with a love for teaching. When you connect with that deep sense of love and joy, you discover your purpose.

But what about passion? Passion is the deeper emotional energy behind your purpose—what lies beneath that specific goal. If you're working out to get rid of the bulge or because you're scared of having a heart attack, you'll only exercise or eat healthy until you feel "safe" again: when you can see your feet again or the doctor gives you a clean bill of health. But what if—bear with me here; I know it will sound crazy—what if you start to love working out? What if you find you love challenging yourself to tackle higher weights or competing against tougher, more experienced opponents or catching that runner's high by breaking past the wall? Now you've got passion. It's like the difference between having a job that pays the bills—a fine purpose—and having a job that both pays the bills *and* brings you joy every time you enter your workplace: the famous "dream job." If purpose is the reason we built our proverbial fire, passion is the bellows making it burn hot and fast.

That spark of motivation that happens on New Year's Eve or when you read a book or get an idea for a business—that's just the start. It helps you to move in a specific direction. Your thoughts might be fixated on all the great things that could happen.

When it came to my business, I daydreamed about waking up, working out, going to my school full of eager, driven students, and having fun teaching all day. It was the idea of doing the thing I loved the most—combining passion and purpose—that made me a better man and able to share that energy with others.

To bring this full circle, I'll use my journey as the example. When I first watched Royce Gracie on that VHS tape, I had an interest—an unlit match. I saw something that I thought would be really cool to be able to do. It wasn't love at first sight. I didn't turn to my fourteen-year-old friend and proclaim, "I will become a black belt and teach this to thousands of students one day." No. I had a deep interest, and that was all.

But then I saw the sport up close in a dojo. The fluid movements and effortless transitions of experienced students struck the match, and I felt motivated to get better. I don't know the exact moment, but somewhere between learning from Alvis and studying under Carlos Machado, I had the notion that teaching was part of my story. BJJ grew beyond just a strong interest; I now had a purpose, a *why*—to make a career of teaching BJJ. And I became passionate about my learning. I loved coming to the mat every day. As the end goal developed, the road that led to it also took shape. Now that I knew what I wanted—my purpose—I had uncovered my passion and found the motivation to follow the long, difficult path involving sacrifice and mat time. Like a committed relationship, it wasn't always easy, but I continued for the love of it.

But what about discipline? Doesn't it take discipline to achieve goals? Maybe you think you don't have enough discipline.

With a strong purpose, we now have a reason to get out of bed even when we feel exhausted. The power of routine kicks in. The initial inspiration and the *why* we found in our purpose created habits, and now those habits help us do the right things like waking up an hour earlier, skipping sugary desserts, and drinking water instead of soda. This is discipline—nothing more than the intentional formation of good habits. At first, discipline is the willingness to scramble for twigs, scraps of paper, or dry grass if the flame starts dying—especially if you're in a frozen wilderness. But once the flame is roaring, all you need is to consistently feed it. And if you've formed good habits, you will. In reality, the longer you do something, the less perceived discipline you need, because it becomes automatic. Alleged "superdisciplined" people are nothing more than people who have consciously chosen beneficial habits over a long period of time. Comparing yourself to them is like comparing someone who can barely curl a five-pound dumbbell to a gold medal weightlifter. The primary difference is that the medalist has been training longer.

I've had people comment on how disciplined I am. I'm not. Like a lot of people, I'm inherently lazy. Most days I'm ready to get going and get things done, but some days I'd rather stay in bed. And some tasks I just hate doing—I don't enjoy working on the accounts or scheduling a marketing plan, for example. But these items have to be done or I won't get to do the things I enjoy: teaching, training, traveling, competing, and mentoring. What makes the difference is that I decide to do a little bit—I just get started for a few minutes—and by doing a little bit, I end up doing more. I set a task in my calendar, I sit down at the computer, and then I just try to work on it for ten minutes. I can do *at least* ten minutes. Next thing I know, it's an hour later and I'm done. Even taking the time to prep ideas and make revisions in this book are less than exciting, but I need to do them. So I just sit down and promise myself to do it for a short time. It's enough of a jumpstart to help me form the habit of doing things I'd rather not.

But let's add a fifth word to our motivation-purpose-passion-discipline list: what's a goal without a deadline? Going back to the example of health, suppose your goal was to lose twenty pounds of fat. You have the purpose of having energy to play with your kids, you've had the discipline to create good habits, and you've brought passion to it. You learned to love working out and finding great-tasting, healthy recipes. But you're losing about a quarter pound a month. That's not necessarily bad, it's progress, but it means something is off. If you have no deadline, you might not take time to look at why your progress is slow.

I love deadlines—deadlines like moving to Brazil, moving home, leaving the garage (a deadline I didn't set, but it was a deadline nonetheless), or registering for a competition before entries close. Deadlines inspire and compel me to take action. I might miss a deadline, and I often do, but I'm always further along than I would have been without one.

Deadlines are tricky. Set them too aggressively, and you won't even try. "Lose twenty pounds of fat by next Tuesday" is unrealistic without surgery. But set them too far into the future, and there's a temptation to procrastinate. In other words, giving yourself five years to lose that weight feels uninspiring, while trying to lose it within a week feels impossible and discouraging. Try to find the Goldilocks zone for your goal's deadline—the one that feels *just right*: motivating, challenging, and inspiring. Ninety-day deadlines are a good place to start. If your goal is to lose a lot of weight—say a hundred pounds—then you can't achieve it all in that time frame. But an intermediate goal to lose thirteen pounds in ninety-days feels achievable; it's only one pound a week.

With a deadline to work backward from, you now can plan what you need to do this week and even tomorrow to move toward your goal. You want to achieve a blue belt by the end of the year? How often do you need to train every week to make that happen? What resources do you need? What core techniques do you need to drill, practice, and master? With a deadline, it all comes into focus, and the plan becomes clear. Maybe it will take a little longer than your deadline, but you're closer to your goal than had you not aimed for any date. As you continue to implement deadlines, you will get better at setting them realistically.

Whatever it is you want to achieve, it's always the bigger reasons— the purpose, the *why*—that will keep you going through the tough times. I recently went through a difficult time that I will discuss a little later. Having a great purpose helped me to eventually come out of it. For me, my purpose comes down to the people in my life. We all make little sacrifices for the ones we love. I love teaching, and the small sacrifices I make to keep doing that are worth it for me. It sustains my deep love for what I get to do. That's what keeps me motivated and passionate, even when I'm exhausted and don't feel like smiling and leading the sixth class of the week. I take a moment and realize I'm doing what I want to do, and then I just start. One minute of smiles and handshakes, and the next thing I know, I'm in the mood to teach another class.

Learn to Love Learning

While committing to the process and making sacrifices are a big part of achieving success, a poor mindset can halt any positive gains. Mindset is your overall attitude and how you think about events in your world, and it can either be your asset or liability.

Many of my students are kids and teenagers. In the past, some have dropped out for a variety of reasons. Sometimes they moved away, chose another sport, or perhaps just lost interest. What's always heartbreaking, however, is when a kid is excited about BJJ but gives up because of poor mindset. Or worse yet, the parent had a poor mindset. On several occasions there was a kid who started and had some decent physical qualities that could help him become great at BJJ. He struggled with learning the basics like most kids do, but he didn't see this as just a simple setback or part of the learning process. Instead, I believe he came to the conclusion that he was bad at BJJ or he sucked at it. A kid might struggle with a basic technique or tap out easily at first. It happens all the time for new students of all ages. What determines his success is whether his mindset sees these mistakes as obstacles to overcome or as something inherently wrong with him. As instructors, we are prepared for this and we take great measures to encourage, motivate, and teach our students. Our teaching style as a school is technical, but when we see a kid get discouraged, we pay attention to the student's individual needs and body language. We teach the value of overcoming the challenges faced on the mat. A young child has not lived long enough to really understand the value of developing this mindset. It comes by way of daily habits and practice. This is where the parents can make a huge positive impact on the child by allowing them to fail, get back up, and try again. However, if they allow the child's bad attitude to govern their decisions, they will give in and allow their child to quit far too early.

On the other side, we have Cameron as an example. Cameron enrolled when he was fourteen years old. Painfully shy and standoffish, Cameron had difficulty socializing with his teammates and was hesitant to ask questions. Over time, he developed a great training mindset.

The learning process was a little slow at first, but he kept trying. When he got taken down, he bounced up and wanted to try again. Whenever he struggled with a move, he practiced it over and over again. Instead of seeing himself as a bad student or bad at jiu-jitsu, he had a mindset to learn and grow and to see setbacks as opportunities to get better. Cameron did get better: class after class, month after month, he put in the required practice and mat time.

Another example of a student who stuck with the program is Anthony Martinez. Anthony began training at my school at the tender age of five. Today he is seventeen, a blue belt, an instructor for our kids' program, and a candidate for the West Point Naval Academy's summer program. A straight A student in all AP-level classes in school, he is a prime example of what can happen when parents nurture a child's passion until that passion becomes a clear vision. Anthony has already mapped out his goals and a detailed plan of action for his future, all while enjoying the present moment every day.

What separates Cameron, Anthony, and all successful martial artists from students who quit too soon is best described in *Mindset*, Dr. Carol Dweck's groundbreaking book. The book outlines our tendency to have one of two mindsets: a fixed mindset or a growth mindset. Succeeding at jiu-jitsu or in business is more about mindset than technique.

A fixed-mindset person believes that things are just the way they are. They were born with certain talents and abilities. This kind of person might struggle with math, say. It could be their learning style or the teacher's approach, but they apply themselves and fail. They might start saying, "I'm not good at math." In a more sinister way, this kind of thinking can damage their identity: "I'm dumb."

On the other side of the spectrum is a growth-mindset person. They also believe they might have some basic talents or abilities, but they see mistakes as opportunities to grow. Given the same situation—struggling with math—a growth-mindset person might fail the first few tests and think, "Hmmm, I'm doing something wrong. Let me ask the teacher or ask for tutoring or watch a video online." A growth-mindset person doesn't believe they're inherently bad, dumb, or incapable. The challenge doesn't define how they see themselves. Instead, they view their identity as separate from their current abilities and decide that they just need more practice, information, or help to improve.

In interviews, Dr. Dweck has admitted that a fixed mindset can be advantageous when it comes to big identity issues like sexuality (knowing who you are and not wavering in doubt) and age (admitting to yourself that you are older and not trying every procedure or scam to stay "youthful"). But overall, researchers have found that it's best to adopt a growth mindset because it frees you to pursue your full potential in every area of life. For more information, I highly encourage you to read the book!

Somewhere along my path, I developed this growth mindset when it came to BJJ and business. I know it's okay to lose a match, get put into a submission I can't get out of, or struggle with a new maneuver. That means I'm learning. That means I have the chance to improve. It's scary when you're always pushing the boundaries of what you know. But that's how the comfort zone got its name—leaving it is uncomfortable!

When you embrace a growth mindset, you begin to see life not as a set of obstacles but as a set of opportunities to stretch, learn, and grow. If you're the best at your level, if you're winning every match or getting 100 percent on every test, then you're not growing. If you're that big a fish, your pond is too small. As scary as it is, that's when it's time to leave your comfortable pond and step into a lake, river, or an ocean.

Though I've developed a growth mindset, I'm still tempted by the comforting thoughts of the fixed mindset—thoughts that wonder why I am wasting my time on this new thing, or tell me I won't ever understand something, or suggest I'm not good enough to overcome this current challenge. For example, I started learning to play guitar in my mid-thirties. Just when I think I'm getting kind of good, my brother plays a lick that reminds me what a real guitar player should sound like. Watching his fingers effortlessly traverse the instrument can feel discouraging, but I remind myself that this all makes sense. He's been playing every day for about twenty years. As I said, I'm more naturally pessimistic. A little healthy pessimism has its place—otherwise every company might become an Enron, where a culture of delusional optimism led to fraudulent reports and destroyed lives—but it's important to not stay in pessimism, or you'll never leave your pond.

When I started the school, I had only a couple of books to help guide me. I was still pretty lost, but those books became buoys in my new ocean to help keep my head above the waves. The habit of self-improvement that Jeremy Trahan had introduced me to seven years earlier helped connect me with my true love and passion for the sport. I continued reading about business and marketing in general as well as inspirational memoirs from athletes, soldiers, and business leaders. In each book I'd highlight the parts that stuck out to me. Sometimes I'd find a marketing idea that I could use right away. Other times I'd discover a shift in thinking that got me to see a challenge from a new perspective. But each book taught me something, and I was a willing student. I refused to see myself as just a bad businessman—I didn't let it become my identity. I strove to keep the perspective that "this is just another skill I don't have yet, but I can learn it."

Like with relationships and goals, there's an element of sacrifice when it comes to learning. Sacrifice is a part of any success. In jiu-jitsu, you must sacrifice time away from leisure activities, hobbies, fun times with friends (although training jiu-jitsu is usually fun with friends), and other activities. If you want to learn about leadership, philosophy, time management, or any subject matter, you will need to invest your time wisely. You may love listening to the radio when driving, but if you utilize that time to listen to an audiobook, it will get you closer to your goal than rocking out to Tool (love those guys). These are the habits that helped carry me higher and are continuing to move me to the next level.

Mastering the Use of Mentors

Mentors have always been essential to my growth in BJJ. Alvis Solis and Carlos Machado were my first two mentors in the sport. A mentor doesn't have to be a world-class expert; he just has to be a couple of steps ahead on the same path. While Alvis was not a black belt when I started training with him back in 1998, he knew so much more than I did and gave me a firm grasp of the basics. Nothing beats having someone experienced look at what you're doing and tell you where you can improve. Carlos Machado was one of the top instructors in the world and a true master of the art. Learning from him was invaluable.

A mentor can't be a substitute for your *why* or your passion and drive, though they can help you find it. In the end, success is entirely up to you and how you respond to setbacks. I knew that having a successful, thriving school—much like the success in achieving a black belt—was up to me. That being said, there's no substitute for mentors. I had them in my BJJ practice, but in the early days of my school, I was missing this key element.

Having a mentor means much more than imitating someone successful. A good coach or mentor can spot your strengths and weaknesses better than you can. Sometimes these truths can be hard to swallow, but if you have a growth mindset and are willing to see suggestions—what you're doing wrong—as an opportunity to improve, you can see dramatic growth in a short period of time.

You can call them mentors, teachers, role models, coaches, gurus—it doesn't matter. Just know that it's more difficult to grow without them and damn near impossible to reach your full potential. I've been blessed with many mentors, including a few that I've yet to discuss, but mentors are not just good-natured souls who are willing to invest time in you because they've got nothing better to do. In most cases, I paid for their guidance. But more than that, when they saw I was committed and took their teaching seriously, they were willing to extend themselves beyond the business relationship. Whether it was Alvis or Carlos who taught and inspired me, or the Gracies who inspired millions and helped bring me to my next level, I've always searched for great teachers. Even today I train under Saulo and Alexandre "Xande" Ribeiro, two amazing jiu-jitsu fighters who have won a combined twelve world championships. Saulo is a powerful coach and mentor, and he radiates a contagious and commanding presence. The technical database of knowledge these two possess, combined with their desire to serve their students, represents the best jiu-jitsu I have ever seen. But besides jiu-jitsu, I'm also invested in a business mastermind group for school owners. In the group, we converse and help each other while learning from industry leaders.

Mentors are available for every area of life and can be found if you're willing to look for them. If you're struggling with leadership in your company, you can hire a top consultant to create a leadership development program for you. But if after three months of working with her, you don't implement any of her advice, she's going to go away. Mentors, even those whose services you're paying for, are interested in spending their time where it will do the most good. You need to demonstrate that you're a willing student who listens and takes action. As one who has mentored others, there's no greater joy than seeing the improvements that follow my student's disciplined efforts. I love watching a dedicated student win a major competition or earn a new belt rank.

It's great to have mentors who inspire you—you can emulate them, you can even imitate them, but you will never be them. You have to be you. It's easy to idolize a jiu-jitsu champion or a leader in your field and model yourself after them. If you want to be a public speaker, you could copy the style and personality of a top motivational speaker. But in both cases, you won't be giving your best, because nobody else is you. No one will move, speak, or think exactly like you; you have to embrace that fact. You can't strive to be somebody else. You'll stifle your growth, and your best self-expression will never emerge.

What you can do is learn the fundamentals. Get a solid understanding of the basics through learning as much as you can and from wherever you can—books, classes, practice—and then allow your mentors and coaches to guide you to your ideal version of yourself. If you want to be a UFC contender, you can imitate Randy Couture all day long. But a coach will come along and tell you, no, you have great fast-twitch muscles in your legs. You could develop a blinding kicking speed that Randy couldn't. Grappling and takedowns might be a weakness you can work on, but why not also build on your strengths?

The Next Steps

Initially, all I wanted was to teach a sport I love. Once I moved into that twelve-hundred-square-foot facility, I had, in theory, achieved my goal. But I was still struggling financially, my relationship was in limbo, and I had yet to find true business mentors. The fact is, every goal is just an illusion. Once you reach that endpoint or even approach its accomplishment, you can then see beyond it.

I dove into the books again. Meanwhile, I continued the kind of advertising I had been using, with the same mediocre results. But my growth mindset didn't allow me to settle for things staying just as they were. Like during my first week in Brazil, when I was put into submission by a paper-cutter hold I had no defense for, I wasn't discouraged; I was excited, because it was something I could learn. I knew of a few martial arts instructors around the country who were succeeding phenomenally. Obviously, they knew something I didn't. I could have resigned myself to thinking they had better breaks or were better teachers or were in better markets or who were just plain smarter, but I didn't. I believed a path to success lay somewhere among these weeds and trees I was lost in. I just needed to find it.

Unfortunately, sometimes the path that looks like it leads to the mountaintop leads to the valley instead.

If you're not failing, you're not pushing your limits, and if you're not pushing your limits, you're not maximizing your potential.

—Ray Dalio[12]

[F]ear doesn't go away. The warrior and the artist live by the same code of necessity, which dictates that the battle must be fought anew every day.

—Steven Pressfield[13]

CHAPTER 6

Failure and Fearlessness

Are you breathing right now? Do you have dreams you want to achieve? Then as long as you continue breathing and pursuing your dreams, you will encounter failure. What you do with that failure will determine whether you continue to progress or give up.

While trudging along the path toward your dreams and goals, you're going to fail. This isn't very motivating, but it's true. Failure is inevitable on the path to success. What baby walks the first time it tries? None. They fall, fall, and fall again. And yet you walk, right? You probably can run, ride a bike, and maybe even drive a stick shift. Every one of these required massive amounts of failure before you got it right. Why would achieving *anything* worthwhile be any different?

Failure is only the end of your dream if you allow it to be. Instead, see failure as a teacher. It's a chance to review what went wrong so you can learn and be better prepared next time. And I believe the sooner you fail, the better. When you get it out of the way, you begin to understand that failure is not the opposite of success; it is the path to success. A good

---

12 Ray Dalio, *Principles: Life & Work* (New York: Simon & Schuster, 2017), 153.

13 Steven Pressfield, *The War of Art: Break through the Blocks and Win Your Inner Creative Battles* (New York: Black Irish Entertainment, 2002), 14.

example of this was my first week in Brazil, when I first experienced that modified paper-cutter choke I had no defense for. I tapped out quickly. But instead of feeling discouraged, I got excited. Here was something new I hadn't learned yet!

Of course I've experienced thousands of little failures in mastering BJJ. It's true of learning anything, whether it's getting answers wrong on a school exam or trying to master the piano. Mastery comes through the willingness to fail and having a level of fearlessness.

You may think of fearlessness as being without fear. That's not my definition. People without fear have a medical condition called Urbach–Wiethe disease (it's true, look it up), and there are only about four hundred known cases. The rest of us? We have a ton of fear. Fear is good. It's trying to keep you safe, keep you from doing something dangerous or painful, regardless of whether that pain is physical or emotional. Paradoxically, fearlessness is not the absence of fear; it's the willingness to lean into and embrace your fear. By leaning into the fear, you risk failure. But by risking failures, you eventually find your successes.

For some reason, this idea of *failing in order to succeed* makes perfect sense to us in sports, music, and education, but we don't apply it to many other situations. Failure has a bad reputation in areas like work, business, finances, and relationships. Working on your free throw and missing ten shots in a row can be frustrating, but if you have a growth mindset and are determined, you stick with it. But can you imagine going to a club or a dance and being rejected by ten attractive people in a row? For most people, that feels devastating. With the free throws, you can examine your hand position, your follow-through, and how square your alignment is to the hoop. But you never see a guy get turned down, then break out a little pencil and notebook and ask himself, "Was it my pickup line or my eye contact? Is it my breath?"

I had no issues with getting slammed into the mat and tapping out again and again and again, but I found it excruciating to muster the courage to approach one girl, Ingrid, in Cicero's just one time. The latter risked no physical pain, but the potential emotional pain—that fear—was very uncomfortable. We humans are a peculiar bunch, aren't we?

The key to overcoming failure is to change your perspective on what failure means to you. Decide in advance that failure is a lesson only and nothing more. This balances the fear with rationality, making it easier to lean into it and become fearless. As with physical training, it takes time to train your mind. Maybe it's best to show you how I overcame some pretty embarrassing mistakes. But first, let's look at how far I got before I took some major risks.

Approaching Normal

Just because I now had a legitimate school location with an office, a bathroom, and a commercial lease, I hadn't yet "succeeded" in the traditional sense, but I felt like I was succeeding. I subscribe to early motivational speaker Earl Nightingale's definition: "Success is the progressive realization of a worthy ideal." In other words, success is defined by progress, and I had definitely made progress. At the same time, I hadn't failed yet either—I hadn't taken too many risks. Funny how not having many failures can seem like a good thing, but in fact the business was just hobbling along. It would take me time to learn that the willingness to take risks and fail in business is what leads to the most growth.

Still, the school was established and new students were finding me. The growth wasn't sensational, but more students equaled increased revenue and more drive behind my purpose. In addition, I'd raised my prices by like twenty bucks a month, which helped. I had a little extra money to reinvest in the business and wasn't worrying as much about life expenses. Besides that, having the opportunity to teach more eager and willing students made it easy to show up each day. I always feel joy bubble up inside of me when I watch my students learn. So I had twofold joy: the ability to pay my bills and help others at the same time. Does it get any better?

It was during this time that I continued to work toward Ingrid's visa as well as visit her in Brazil while lugging a few accordions with me every few months. Between that and working with Dr. Luu on my slowly improving herniated disc, I felt like things were going well for a change—that I could actually make this business work.

At the same time, though, I was still sleeping on a comforter on the floor of my dad's house. I had my own bedroom, but I knew this was no place to bring my future wife. I was paying my bills, yes, but I had a desire to grow my business. I wanted to make a comfortable living, and I also had a desire to provide for Ingrid. Maybe it's sexist, but I think there's a need hardwired in men to provide for their partner, and I was not in a strong position to provide.

Other than my desire to provide, I was content. I've never equated money with happiness. Ever since I was sixteen and wanted to be either a martial artist or a Navy SEAL, I didn't see a college education and the big salary it's supposed to buy you as being a realistic part of my life's equation. There's nothing wrong with pursuing and obtaining an education as long as it's what you want. I've seen many people work to get the grades they need to get accepted into a great college, which they believe will lead to a good career and lots of money. That's great. I'm all for college if you want to be a doctor, engineer, or another vocation that requires a degree. I'm also all for pursuing education for the sake of education itself, if that's what you really want. If you believe you'd love doing that, go for it.

The problem exists in thinking that some undefined "great job" and, above all, a high salary will create happiness. Not necessarily. Actually, it's often the opposite. Numerous studies have confirmed that having enough money to pay for basic necessities—mortgage, health care, food—does alleviate worries and therefore can provide a higher level of happiness. But beyond that point, more money usually doesn't get you anything other than a bigger bank account. And suppose you achieve that magical "no worries" income level but are working sixty to seventy hours a week in a job you hate. Are you really happy then? Not likely. Hedonic adaptation quickly sets in. What that means is that somewhere around $75,000 (depending on the cost of living where you are), happiness from more money peaks. Science is telling us what we've been saying for centuries: beyond a certain point, more money alone will not buy happiness.

So if you're pursuing the big salary and corner office because you think it will make you happy, don't. It won't. If you have a choice between money and life experience, choose the life experience.

This doesn't mean you have to go full hippie, either, and live a life without money. You need to find a balance, and you have to figure out what that is for you. I do want to acknowledge the importance and value of money. As the saying goes, "Money isn't everything, until you don't have any." In fact, I love pursuing my financial goals (and they are big), but I have also attached value-based goals and objectives to my financial goals. This combination gives the art of making money greater meaning.

I didn't pursue my black belt to make money. I pursued my black belt to master the art I love and make a living teaching it to others. I was making progress on my worthy ideal. Making a *comfortable* living was another matter, one that required risks and mistakes. Oh boy, did I make some mistakes.

Mistake One: Having the Wrong Mentors

By the time I'd left my dad's garage, I was getting well-connected within the martial arts community, but I hadn't yet created any relationships in the business world. So meeting a business mentor over a cup of coffee to discuss strategy and marketing wasn't an option, but I needed help, so I found a business mentor group. I don't remember how I found them exactly—probably googling "business help" late one night when I was trying to figure out what I was doing—although this was before *google* was a verb, so I don't really recall the details—and I clicked on their banner ad.

I thought this group might be exactly what I needed. They bragged about their years of experience in various businesses and their full complement of knowledgeable consultants, and offered an intimate coaching program. Wow, for only $500 a month, I'd get all of this. I say *only*, but it was almost half my revenue (excluding private lessons) at that time and was barely doable. My monthly take was a whopping $1,200 when I signed up, but I figured if they could help me double that, it'd be worth every penny. At least, that's what they told me. I suppose the desire to grow was so strong that I ignored the details.

They sent me a bunch of materials—CDs and DVDs—and I remember when I had the first call with the mentor. I'd gotten the confirmation email and we set an appointment. I was by the phone watching the seconds tick away until the appointed time, eager for this life-changing call.

My coach was knowledgeable, professional, and even likable. I'm happy to say they weren't a scam. The first call went great, but I didn't understand everything he was talking about. Around the fifth call, I had that uneasy feeling in the pit of my stomach that this wasn't a great fit. The guy started talking about profit and loss, marketing mix, upselling; my head was buzzing with terms. Sure, I knew some of those terms, but I'd only begun to understand what they meant. The info was good, but it was not what I needed at that time. I felt like I was a white belt learning black belt techniques—I wasn't ready. Unfortunately, it took me a few weeks of calls before I'd realized they weren't a good match for my business.

Not for one minute do I regret signing with the program, though. Even though it was a bad fit for me, and they didn't understand a martial arts business model, it was a valuable experience. It taught me that I was on the right track, and it confirmed that I needed to take these types of risks in order to grow and that I'd have to be willing to risk losing in order to gain. So that's what I kept doing.

Mistake Two: Believing a Smooth-Talking Salesman

The full sweltering Houston heat had returned that summer of '06, and my school was expanding. I'd lose a student now and then, but each month I'd have one or two students more on the roster than I had the month before, which meant I was growing, albeit slowly.

When you're in close proximity with a student week after week, it's easy to develop a fondness and even friendship. Sometimes students would drop out for a variety of reasons. This was understandable but still a little disappointing. Then sometimes they'd leave for another martial arts school. That felt a bit like betrayal in the beginning. Emotions and thoughts would flood my mind, taking me on a tidal ride from blaming the student to wondering if I was a good teacher. It was emotionally taxing. When this would happen, I'd take a breath and remind myself of what I knew to be true—that most of these mental stories are not the truth; they're just my version of the truth. To master your emotions, you must use logic and rational thinking. You must learn to separate the truth of what happens to you from the emotional drama created by your inner voice. We tell ourselves stories all the time. They make us feel good, they can make us feel miserable and every emotion in between. Objective focus with a bit of extra faith in what you're working for has proven to be a winning formula over the years.

While I was getting used to the revolving door of students, one student took me on an emotional ride I'll never forget. For the sake of the story, let's call this student Adam to protect his identity.

Adam became a student in the late spring. A car salesman, he'd often come to the morning classes since those worked best for his schedule. These classes are usually smaller, so we had a lot of one-on-one time together.

Adam *looked* and *sounded* like a car salesman. But that wasn't necessarily a bad thing. I certainly don't want to discredit the profession of selling or salesmen. The title of salesperson is pretty badass and too often gets a bad rap in society. It's a storied profession full of many hardworking people with integrity. But Adam wasn't such a person. I'd like to say that all I did was buy a lemon from him—it would've been less expensive.

Because we'd spent a lot of time together over that spring and summer, we'd grown close, as I have with many students. One day he approached me with a lucrative idea.

"Have you ever thought about hosting your own tournament?" Adam asked.

That sounded interesting. I'd refereed at a few tournaments over the years and helped others organize them, but I'd never really toyed with the idea of hosting one myself. I knew it was a lot of work to put one together. He had my attention, save for the doubt in my mind.

"No," I finally said. "I don't think I'm interested in doing that right now."

One thing a good salesman does is target your hot buttons. Whether he knew I was barely getting by, or he merely chose his own button, I don't know, but that's how he got my attention.

"I work for this car company," he continued, "and they're always looking to sponsor events like these. I'd bet I could get them to give you ten or twenty grand to be the main sponsor of a big jiu-jitsu tournament. On top of that, I have a friend at Reliant Arena. I could get us in there for basically free."

Now if you're not a football fan, you might not know what Reliant Arena is. Today it's called NRG Arena, and it's the home of the Houston Texans NFL team. The place is amazing in its size and beauty, complete with a massive overhead retractable skylight. It seats almost seventy-two thousand people. Of course, we weren't going to have the competition in the same part of the venue where they play the games but in a subsection that was still enormous! Big sponsorship, low overhead, and one hell of a venue—Adam painted the picture with broad, colorful strokes. For some reason, the adage "If it sounds too good to be true, it probably is" never entered my mind.

"Holy crap, that's unbelievable!" I'm not sure if I said it or merely thought it, but it's the statement that sticks with me. I wish I'd paid attention to the *unbelievable* portion.

But as he continued, he kept repeating one word: "guaranteed." Like "This is a guaranteed profit center," or "I guarantee you can't lose on this," or "I guarantee I can get you a free arena and $10,000." I'm sure he believed what he was saying. After all, his only request was free training for himself, so it wasn't like he stood to make any big bucks on the whole thing.

We hashed out the details, and I developed a plan for the event over the ensuing months. By late summer, here's what I thought would happen: I'd bring in some of the best grapplers—the big names for super fights, exclusive one-on-one matches separate from the main tournament to draw in crowds. Then we'd have a proper tournament with various matches. I'd get about $25,000 in free rent for the stadium, plus up to $20,000 in sponsors' money. Add to that ticket sales, tournament entry fees, and concessions, and we're talking some serious revenues. We'd offer a total in prize money of $8,000. After expenses like insurance, stipends for the referees and judges, refreshments, facility fees and such, I'd be sitting on a pretty decent take. By the time the competition arrived, we had lined up for the super fights of Marcelo Garcia, Rafael Lovato Jr., Romulo Barral, Mike Fowler, Ryan Hall, Bill Cooper, and Justin Rader, just to name a few. What made it even better was that Ingrid's visa had finally been approved (after my major screwup on her paperwork), and she might make it just in time to see my tournament, which was scheduled for that November. What could go wrong?

Here's where late radio personality Paul Harvey would tell "The rest of the story."

All That Glitters . . .

Adam was the key to making this happen. The fast-talking salesman had the connections at the car company and the stadium. So I went ahead and scheduled the competitors, reserved the venue, and printed flyers, even though I didn't have any sponsorship money yet or confirmation for the venue. As long as Adam stayed in the mix, this was going to be the biggest payout opportunity for the growth of my career, "guaranteed."

Except Adam didn't stay in the mix.

Instead, Adam left the mix because he was too busy navigating through a mid-life crisis where his dishonesty finally caught up to him. Before the tournament, he left the car company he was working for to work for another car company. In the midst of his career change, he also managed to have an affair with a nineteen-year-old girl, which led to his divorce.

"Oh, I'm sorry man," he explained to me when I finally got him on the phone four weeks before the tournament. "I'm out of the loop on that stuff. I can't get you that sponsorship anymore. And my life's been crazy."

"But you guaranteed—"

"Well . . . I can guarantee that my new company will offer you five or six grand" (which never happened either), "but I can't get you anything from that other one."

I was freaking out. The money I'd planned the tournament's budget around was gone, and there was no way I could change the payout amounts or the venue at this point. Everything was already set, the flyers were printed, and the competitors for the main event were lined up. I was stuck.

In the end, when November arrived, what was supposed to be a big net windfall of fifty to sixty grand turned into a net loss of about twelve grand, even after collecting over three hundred competitor registration fees. On top of that, Ingrid arrived two days after this fiasco, still a little pissed off about my screwing up on her paperwork. It was a definite low point for me.

There was no way I could cover the shortfall, as my monthly revenue had only increased to around $3,000 with roughly thirty-five students, so I had to secure a bank loan, which my father cosigned for, thankfully. Fortunately, I got the loan before the event, so I could pay the vendors and winners.

Do I blame Adam? I can't, if I'm being honest. I trusted his word and got nothing in writing. As the saying goes, "A verbal contract is worth the paper it's written on." I had no written commitments, no protection to cover me just in case. I'm the only one to blame.

As I've said before, the stories we tell ourselves matter. I had to decide to frame the events in a way that served me, not hurt me. As Tony Robbins says, "Where focus goes, energy flows," and I didn't want all my energy directed at negativity. I could've stayed angry with Adam, resentful over the lost money, and vow to never trust anyone ever again. But where would that get me? It would only hurt me.

Instead, I decided to focus on what I could learn from this—remember growth mindset? Besides, the memories from the super fights of that event are still talked about to this day: the overtime match between Rafael Lovato Jr. and Romulo Barral, Romulo running through the no-gi division to capture gold, and Marcelo Garcia and Rafael Lovato Jr. fighting the finals of the gi super fight division—amazing matches! In the end, I learned a few valuable lessons: always get an agreement in writing, tread into relationships a little more lightly, and keep a sharp eye on spending. After all, I had a sizable loan to pay back in addition to my rent, so my budget had to be tighter than it was before.

But this wasn't the end of my risk-taking. I couldn't be paralyzed by the fear of screwing up again. I had to lean into the fear.

In the midst of mistakes, however, I did have some things go my way.

Moving on Up

Though I had a lot of early setbacks, some things did go my way; otherwise, I might not be writing this book. Not long after the tournament disaster, Steve Sanford, the judo instructor and my landlord, approached me with a proposition.

"Travis," he said. "You seem like you're pretty good at managing the business side of the school." (Even though I didn't feel that way at all.) "All I want to do is teach. I hate the bookkeeping, billing, and payroll, and you seem ambitious. How would you like to rent my space?"

I'll remind you that my section of this building was around twelve hundred square feet. The judo school side was around five thousand square feet, over four times bigger. It was an intimidating proposal, and once again I started doing math in my head. I'd obviously be paying more for rent and a little more for utilities . . .

But then he sweetened the deal.

"Let me teach my club under your roof," he continued, "and you can collect all the monthly dues."

I'd just gotten into debt and tightened my finances, but I'd seen a growth spurt in my first move out of the garage. And I trusted Steve. He'd gone out on a limb with our leasing agreement, and I honored it no matter how tight money got. I knew he was a painter by trade—and a judoka (judo player) at heart with a passion for teaching. But he no longer had the desire to grow an academy. The judo thing was more of a social club than a school—a bunch of judo aficionados getting together to practice their art, so I understood why he disliked the business side.

It was a deal. It turned out that the electric and heating bills weren't "a little" higher like I'd thought, but about six times higher, so that was interesting. But with the added revenues from his students, the only trick was setting the schedule to accommodate both of our class schedules, but we made it work. There was only one downside: Steve rented out my old studio to a Pentecostal Church. If you're unfamiliar with how they conduct their services, a KISS concert might have been quieter.

My student roster grew, the quality of what we offered increased, and I decided to take a risk and raise the tuition to ninety-nine dollars a month.

In the meantime, Ingrid and I had a small courtroom wedding, and my cash flow increased once again as new students and the increased tuition poured in. Having a little more money in the coffers meant the opportunity to take some more risks.

Maybe I should have been more timid about trying new things, but I was beginning to understand that business is not unlike training in BJJ. You have to keep a positive mindset and believe, with an intentional faith, that there is a way to make things better. You don't ignore the failures, because they're rich with lessons. But you learn the lessons, then move forward.

If it hasn't already, life will toss you a lot of unfair bullshit to deal with. Bad people will try to take advantage of you, or you'll just make some poor decisions. If you spend more time complaining about rather than navigating through these problems, you'll never rise above them. A loss or a mistake doesn't define your character. The best jiu-jitsu champions get right back to work after a loss. They know making mistakes is how you get better.

I was ready to make more mistakes.

Mistake Three: Advertising to Nobody

If you're placing an advertisement, whether it's a radio or television commercial or a print ad, you would expect somebody to see it, right? That's what I expected, too. Turns out our expectations don't always come true.

Ingrid had arrived, and we had married and settled down in my father's house. There we were, the happy young couple, reunited after being on separate continents for well over a year, sleeping on my old comforter on the floor of a small bedroom. Actually, the comforter lasted
about a week; she made me get a real, human bed after that. Ah, that
was the life. At least I knew she loved me, because she certainly didn't
marry me for my money.

My school continued to grow as I continued to pay off the tournament failure. I had enough cash flow to try reinvesting in the business
again. I chose to invest in a newsletter published by marketing guru Dan
Kennedy. This was a *good* investment.

Dan has been in the trenches of his own businesses and, later, con-
sulting with numerous companies and entrepreneurs creating incredible marketing plans. Every month I'd receive a newsletter packed with
marketing gold and zero fluff. Throughout all the strategies, tactics, and
ideas was Dan's consistent message: you've got to have brass balls when
it comes to business and marketing. I took that message to heart. I decided I was going to take risks and not let fear stop me.

Of course, I was still young and naïve, and I had to allow myself to
make stupid mistakes. Eventually I'd figure it out. Mistakes are great
teachers, unless you have the foresight to see other people who screwed
up and you are smart enough to avoid the same pitfalls. They say, "A smart
man learns from his mistakes, but a wise man learns from the mistakes
of others." I guess I was getting smart. Wisdom would still take some
time. I know I had some foresight to learn from others, but I still believe
that making big mistakes is a better way to go than being overly cautious.

On the heels of the tournament loss, with my new, figurative brass
balls, I had an idea to reach out to a younger crowd. I hadn't learned yet
about focusing your marketing efforts and tailoring them to a specific
audience. My idea was to set up an information booth with brochures
and free passes in a movie theater's lobby. I had heard that this was a
popular method to attract new students, so I decided to give it a go. Eager
to move forward, I made an appointment with the theater's salesperson.

When I sat down with Beth, I had one goal in mind: get permission
or pay to set up that booth for one night. Beth, with her coifed blonde
hair, was poised and seemed eager to help me have a greater impact.

She leaned across her desk. "Why set up a booth for only one night," she asked, "when you can get in front of thousands of people every single day?" She then explained how ads played before movies worked.

I hadn't thought about that. It made perfect sense to me.

"Here's what we can do," she offered. "We can run your commercial before every movie in this theater. You have a potential of reaching a captive audience of tens of thousands!"

It sounded good. Even a low conversion rate would send dozens of new students to my school. "How much would this cost?"

"Over three months, and dozens of showings a day"—she punched numbers into her desk calculator—"Fifteen thousand dollars."

I thought I was having a heart-attack. "Fifteen—"

"But we can break that payment up." She must have seen my pupils dilate to the size of quarters. "You can pay an installment every month over the course of the six months."

Brass balls—I had to lean into the fear. Then I did some math. Suppose out of five thousand movie goers I only converted 1 percent? That's fifty new students at a hundred dollars a month or almost sixty grand a year in new revenue. That's a 300 percent return on investment. Sold! Beth printed up the paperwork, I signed it, and two weeks I later provided my commercial that I had a specialist create.

Over the next few weeks, it was like me hanging the little wooden signs on telephone poles all over again. I waited for the new prospective students to call or drop by. They never did. I was getting nervous. Was my commercial being shown?

But I had a few reports. "Hey, I saw your commercial. It was pretty good," a student said. A few more confirmed that they'd seen the commercial before the movie. Well, at least it was airing. But where were the new students? Had I screwed up on the telephone number or the address? I was pretty sure I hadn't, as I had meticulously checked those details.

Finally I popped in for a movie one day to see for myself. I arrived extra early just to get a peek at my masterpiece on the big screen. I entered the theater where one young crew member was still cleaning up after the previous showing.

"Oh, you can't come in here yet!" the cleaning girl barked at me.

"Oh, sorry." I was a little taken aback, but I hid off to one side so I could watch the screen. Sure enough, in between the ads for insurance and Coca-Cola there was the ad for Team Tooke Brazilian Jiu-Jitsu. Instead of thousands, it had an audience of two, the teenage janitor and me. By the time people actually started filling the seats, the ad never ran again. But worse, I realized that my tiny ad was in the company of Fortune 500 giants. These companies had the budget to run ads like this for nothing more than brand awareness. I was a few million dollars short of having a budget for Disney-level brand awareness. I felt absolutely crushed and misled.

That afternoon I wrote a long, sarcastic email to Beth. I was furious. I don't remember everything I wrote, but I do remember saying something to the effect of, "Had I known that the commercial would only be seen by the seventeen-year-old girl scraping sticky popcorn off the floor, I would have saved my fifteen grand and just handed her a brochure."

But Beth was in sales and not marketing. She wrote me back apologizing for the lack of response and did everything she knew how to do to make things better. And it wasn't like no one was seeing the ad, just that the ad's rotation didn't always mean it was getting in front of people. She extended my contract a couple of months and had the commercial show more frequently when she could. In retrospect, I realize she was only doing her job: selling advertising spots for the theater. I feel she truly believed everything she had told me—that I was going to get a bunch of new students by showing my commercial—and in the end I think she felt awful that I didn't get the results I'd hoped for. There are a lot of charlatans in the world, but Beth isn't one of them.

No, the responsibility fell on me . . . again. This is my business. I took a risk, and when the dust settled, I only enrolled two students for my $15,000 investment. Like all failures, this was a hard blow, but I chose to look for the lesson, which was to understand the audience you're advertising to.

At the time, my ideal audience (at least, in my mind) was somewhere between mid-teens to thirty years old, middle class, mostly male, who care about health and fitness, and have an interest in self-defense, MMA, or fighting. I should've focused equally on families and kids in that mix, but I didn't know that yet. My commercial shouted "MMA and Fighting" and only whispered "kids' classes and family friendly." It showed clips of grappling, choking, hard-hitting, fast-kicking intensity with about four seconds of kids running around in their gis. It's like I was target shooting, but instead of aiming with a scoped rifle, I was shooting a shotgun blindfolded.

Avoiding the Worst Mistake

From a business perspective, I've made many mistakes, tried hundreds of ideas, and spent tens of thousands of dollars that have yielded a near-zero return. Those moments are heartbreaking. But success is all about making progress on that worthy ideal. Successful people aren't super-heroes with otherworldly powers; they're simply people who decide every day to get up and keep going no matter what obstacles they come up against.

These massive mistakes were just the mat time I needed to put in as a businessman. I think back to that paper-cutter choke in Brazil. Imagine if I thought, "I don't have a defense for this. I guess I'm not as good as I thought," tapped out, and never returned to class. Who knows where I'd be? Instead I tried again, and again, and again. I learned new counter-tactics, and I quickly learned to defend against that choke.

Sure, you feel disappointed. We're emotional beings. We have to learn to accept the lows with the highs. Feel the disappointment, frustration, and even anger and express those emotions fully. Just don't dwell there.

It's the same with business as it is with life. When we understand that failure is vital to growth and that the only way to find success is to persist despite the failures, we will achieve great success despite setbacks or lack of talent. You must always be willing to learn, try, fail, make adjustments, and try again. Next time you try, you'll feel fear. Lean into the fear. Remember, fearlessness is just the willingness to experience the fear and move forward anyway.

In the end, you don't ever fail as long as you keep learning from your failures. The only way a person becomes a "failure" is when they stop trying. That's the only true failure.

A win is a step forward, and a loss is a lesson for your future. If you're winning, you don't stop and get comfortable there; if you're losing, you don't sit still and stagnate. Never regret the effort you put into something just because you didn't get desired results. Effort is never wasted.

I'd have many more steps forward to come and more losses as well—some I couldn't have ever predicted. My school had grown in number and floor space, but I wasn't done learning and putting in mat time.

Being wrong opens us up to the possibility of change.
Being wrong brings the opportunity for growth.

—Mark Manson[14]

Even in the growth mindset, failure can be a painful
experience. But it doesn't define you. It's a problem to
be faced, dealt with, and learned from.

—Carol Dweck, PhD[15]

CHAPTER 7

Growth and Goofs

I want you to imagine something. Picture what your life would be like if you achieved every single dream you've ever had. Got that image in your head? Now try this: what if everything that could go wrong in your life did go wrong all at once? Lastly, reflect on what your life would be like if you continued down the path you're on and never changed a thing. Overwhelmed by all the *what ifs* yet?

The human brain is a pretty complex and funny thing. An antelope isn't in a state of high anxiety trying to avoid the next lion attack. It's eating grass, looking for mates, and trying to find water. If they encounter a lion, *then* they have anxiety—adrenaline coursing through their veins. If they live, they make a note to avoid that spot where they met said kitty cat, and then they go on eating, mating, and drinking without a care in the world.

Humans, on the other hand, have this wonderfully screwy thing called a prefrontal cortex. It's what allows us to dream, plan, note the passage of time and seasons, and envision future projects and our future selves.

---

14 Mark Manson, *The Subtle Art of Not Giving a F*ck: A Counterintuitive Approach to Living a Good Life* (New York: Harper Collins, 2016), 119.
15 Carol S. Dweck, *Mindset: The New Psychology of Success* (New York: Ballantine Books, 2006), 33.

It's also what allows us to wonder *what if?* Asking *what if*, like many of the brain's higher functions, is a good thing. Without the capacity to ask this—to both foresee dangers and envision solutions—our caveman forebears might never have left the safety of the fire circle (or had a chance to).

But *what if* always has a flipside. Just like with our antelope friend, the fear reaction can keep us from harm. But if we overthink fear, it can also cause us to become shut-ins, spiraling into anxiety. On the other hand, *what if* can be a tool for wonder and creativity—or trap us in an eternal loop of delusional wishful thinking.

Asking *what if* with the wrong motivation or emotion can make us blind to areas where we might improve and grow. The brain always devises an answer to any question you ask it, whether the question is valid or not. Ask, "How come I do stupid things?" or "How come I'm so brilliant?" and it will engender answers to both. Asking the wrong *what if* charged with positive or negative emotion can paralyze us so we avoid the possibility of screwing up or making a mistake or even minor goofs. We sit still, never leaving the fire circle.

The question served me well early on when I asked it with curiosity and a little optimism. I'd wonder, "What if I could get really good at jiu-jitsu?" or "What if I could make a living with my own school and teach and train every day?" Later on, after I thought I'd finally figured everything out, the same *what if* question nearly sunk me.

Moving on Up Again

Prior to the tournament debacle at Reliant Arena, one of my students, Corey, offered to put a website together for me. After all, this was the twenty-first century, and here I was two years in business without a website. Corey was great with web development and helped me launch teamtooke.com in late 2006. The site was simple by today's standards: a black title bar with "Definitive Martial Arts" in a bold red font with gold outlines, and on either side, the double-T logo—an early iteration of the same logo we have today. It wasn't a beautiful site, but at least it didn't have fireworks and dancing banana gifs. It did the trick. More students started coming in and checking us out.

As the school grew, I added more classes and enlisted my friend and student Jeremy Trahan to help me teach the newer classes. I now had children's classes and was beginning to separate introductory classes from the main class. Meanwhile, Steve continued teaching his judo classes under the same roof.

Although I had to repay that loan my dad cosigned to cover the losses from the tournament, the actual loss was less than I had anticipated. Other than the financial shortfall, the tournament was still fairly successful for the participants, and it was fun—even with all my stress.

The loan for the shortfall was secured prior to the event, and I had money left over after all the invoices were paid. Instead of paying it back to the bank right away, I continued making monthly payments so I could build up my credit score and stashed the balance of funds in a separate account. Though it could have been worse, in the end I lost a total of about $12,000. Ouch. With the new enrollments, consistent marketing, and keeping my living expenses ridiculously low, I was able to pay off that loan within a short period of time. All this happened while Ingrid and I, newlyweds, were still sharing that bedroom in my dad's house. That was about to change.

With the extra money I had put away and with us keeping our living expenses to a bare minimum, we purchased our first home in July 2007—an attractive fifteen-hundred-square-foot home in a quiet neighborhood. Had we waited one more year, we would have experienced the fallout from the bursting housing bubble. Prices fell, sure, but we also wouldn't have qualified for a mortgage under the stricter requirements. For us, the timing couldn't have been more perfect.

I'd come a long way from that closet of a bedroom in Brazil. Beyond just having our own place, it felt great to give Ingrid a home to settle into so we could begin our new life together. After the move, we continued keeping our expenses as low as possible so we could pay off the mortgage. I hated being in debt, something that still bothers me today, and did everything I could to cut costs.

I'd grown as a businessman in the meantime and had gotten better at marketing. I'd matured from the telephone pole signs, though I still continued to use them. I had implemented a variety of approaches I learned from Dan Kennedy's newsletter, including buying Google Ads and enhancing with my site's search engine optimization (SEO) so I could show up on the first page of search results as often as possible. Students weren't pouring in, but we had a steady stream of people interested in the free classes. Some of them even decided to stay. At the time, I thought the goal was getting them in the door, and I was doing that. Keeping them there was another matter. Still, enough students stayed to keep all the lights on and my one employee paid, with enough left over to put away for future investments. Things were on an upward trend.

In 2008, things continued to get better. Most memorable was awarding my first black belt. Tom Dinklage—the same man whose school I had once competed in as a teenager and who then later asked me to help him continue his jiu-jitsu training back when I was in my dad's garage—had demonstrated that he was not only technically skilled in BJJ but also highly skilled as a teacher. His graduation to black belt was one of my proudest moments. He had achieved high ranks in other disciplines and was a jiu-jitsu purple belt when we trained together in the garage, but he hadn't settled on a coach to help him continue his BJJ training. So though I hadn't taught him from white belt, it was an incredible feeling to get to tie on his black belt—the honor was overdue.

· · ·

Earlier that same year I met two students who would later become two of my best friends. It can be difficult maintaining that fine line between coach and friend—a line I advise my coaches to avoid crossing as much as possible. Our philosophy is to be friendly with the students, always be there for them, but remain their coach. Talking about school, sports, politics, and work before or after class is one thing. Getting hammered together at a bar on a Saturday night is quite another. When that line is crossed, you risk losing the ability to be a good coach—you're no longer their mentor; you're a casual friend.

When Miguel Castro walked through my door, he had a natural smile and sense of humor that told me he'd be an exception. Already well-versed in various grappling-style martial arts, he had to stop training when his job relocated him out of town in the late '90s. He was a construction project manager for a large mobile service provider. We got to talking one day, and I learned that he constructed the cell tower in my dad's backyard (my dad had leased the land). He had worked right behind where my school started!

Miguel learned the mechanics of jiu-jitsu quickly. His previous jiu-jitsu training, though limited, proved to be a solid foundation to build on. Because of his job, he had the flexibility to show up for day classes, which he did—almost every single day. I used to joke with him, saying, "I don't think you have a real job. All you do is train!"

At that time, I thought he was a really cool guy and an excellent student. Our friendship soon blossomed. Little did I know how instrumental he'd be to my personal and professional life in the future.

Another young man (three years my junior) started training with me that same year. Todd Moore and I connected at a local competition.

"You and I wrestled in high school," he told me.

It took me a minute to place him, but then I remembered him clearly. My school didn't offer wrestling until my senior year while he was wrestling at a rival school as a freshman. When I had wrestled him as a senior, I won, but at one point he had succeeded in getting me into a *back mount*—a jiu-jitsu position where he wrapped his legs around my waist from behind. It's not a scoring position in wrestling, but it is in BJJ. It bugged me that this freshman—a "kid"—was able to do that to me.

When we got reacquainted at my school, he was already a successful professional fighter, but he wanted to expand his BJJ repertoire. I welcomed the chance to train a motivated martial artist of his caliber as much as he welcomed the opportunity to improve his groundwork. Today, Professor Todd is a black belt and one of the head coaches of our Muay Thai kickboxing and beginner jiu-jitsu classes.

• • •

While things were going well, I still had the normal problems of a business owner, and I still had to manage my herniated disc, though that was accomplished mostly with yoga and physical therapy with Dr. Luu by now. But minor everyday problems and annoyances were nothing compared with some of the major mistakes that almost ruined my business.

In October of that year, two exciting things happened: Jace Pitre, one of my original "garage days" students, made his mixed martial arts (MMA) debut; and I opened our second location.

Jace won his match at the forty-three second mark of round one when his opponent submitted after Jace brilliantly executed a rear naked choke.

The second school was located ten miles farther north in Spring, Texas. If you've never been to Houston, the city is huge! It's not only the fourth-largest city by population but also number nine on the list of largest cities by land area in the US, coming in a hair under six hundred square miles. Spring is a small suburb—tiny when compared to Houston—that lies just north of the city. There was a fledgling traditional martial arts school operating there that I partnered with at first, paying half the rent, before I eventually separated from the owner. It seemed like a good risk to take at the time. The new name was Team Tooke Spring. Once again, I was feeling like, "Okay, I've finally got this business thing figured out." And once again, I was wrong.

Another Location—Sort Of

When 2009 rolled around, I was staying afloat, doing the best I could with what I knew. Meanwhile, Miguel Castro, who by then had become a close friend, was quickly advancing. He had already made it to blue belt, and I don't play favorites. If anything, I might be a tad stricter with students I feel close to in order to avoid the appearance of favoritism. Miguel was just a relentless trainer. When he'd make a mistake, he intensely practiced the correction until he got it right. He has the mindset of a master. He would even go on to win the gold medal in the brown belt division of the 2013 IBJJF World Jiu-Jitsu No-Gi Championship.

Miguel had a drive and passion for BJJ equal to my own, and his job continued giving him the flexibility to train as long as he made up the time. That was about to change. The Great Recession was firmly in place and everybody was affected, including Miguel. His company decided to "restructure," which is fancy corporate lingo for "lay people off." He was one of the casualties, but at least they gave him a decent severance package.

After the layoff, he wasn't sure what he wanted to do. Then one day he started asking me a bunch of questions about my business, and I asked why.

"I think I'd like to open up my own school. I'd continue training—I wouldn't be competition . . . I'd open it far enough away that it wouldn't impact you at all."

I felt a wellspring of pride in my heart that my friend wanted to follow his dream of being a school owner. He was technically proficient in jiu-jitsu, though still a blue belt at the time. During his tenure, he had started teaching beginner classes. The students loved him. The idea of mentoring him in business made perfect sense.

By the spring of 2009, he had found a location in Cypress, a small community northwest of Houston and about fifteen miles from my school. Team Tooke Cypress opened its doors in a cozy twelve-hundred-square-foot studio in May of that year. Though it was wholly Miguel's school, we had come to an agreement regarding the use of my name, just as I did with Jace. As a project manager, he had great people skills, but he needed help with business skills. He continued to train with me, and I mentored him in business, though I was only a business blue belt myself—I still had many more mistakes to learn from.

A Flood of Nothing

We fared well through the Great Recession. Some students chose to leave because of job loss or difficult circumstances; others we were able to work out payment agreements or temporary payment freezes so they could keep coming. Despite the recession, we maintained a decent rate of growth, which I was proud of.

Two years later, and the Spring location was staying viable under the capable leadership of Jeremy Trahan. A few months earlier, in early 2010, we had left the partnership in Spring and opened our own location three miles closer to the highway. We had outgrown the partnership with the other school, and it was time to move forward. This new location was much more expensive to operate, though. Some months the main location helped the Spring location with cash flow.

The second location in Spring was smaller than our main location, but at least it was on a main road with a good amount of traffic. I couldn't say the same for our main school. Our enrollment seemed to have plateaued a bit. When I last moved to a larger location, we enrolled more students. And visibility was terrible at that location. Steve never did all that well at that location, either. He was a full-time painter, and judo was more of a hobby he ran on the side. It was tucked off the main road behind a Chevron gas station in the Kleinbrook neighborhood. "What if," I wondered, "I had more visibility and a larger location?" After all, I was a fully developed entrepreneur by this point *cough*.

With a lot of businesses still in recovery mode at the time, it was a renter's market. I began searching and found an ideal space. Where the previous location was hidden behind the gas station, this one was in a strip mall just off a main route, with lots of visibility. There was an O'Reilly Automotive Parts next door, for crying out loud. Not only was the location in a high-traffic location, but it was three thousand square feet larger. While it was a renter's market, I'd still have to pay a premium for this premium spot. My rent would increase from $2,500 to $7,500 a month. But I'd negotiated to get the first six months rent-free and a $35,000 build-out allowance, a reimbursement from the landlord to change the building to fit my needs.

In May of 2010, we opened the doors to the new location. The marketing efforts continued through a consistent mixture of different approaches. If there's one thing I learned through my early mistakes, it's that consistency is key when it comes to marketing. And it worked. New students were flooding in. It seemed like every week the ads, coupons, signs, and everything else were sending a score of new students to our doors. Plus, we were in a much better and more visible location. My idea had worked! I was this close to patting myself on the back. Any worries I had about making the new rent when it came due in November all but vanished.

But things didn't always go smoothly. With so many new prospects coming through the door, tracking them became a logistical nightmare. A lot of new names, faces, and no system to keep track of their information: their first class date, whether they received a gi, if anyone talked to them about enrolling. We had never dealt with that level of traffic and didn't know the best way to handle it. It was happy chaos.

"Hey, did you talk to that guy with the ponytail in the pink shirt?" a coach asked me.

"No. Should I have?"

"Yeah, he's really interested."

"What's his phone number?"

"Uh, not sure. I don't think we have it."

"Okay, then. I'll try to remember next time he's here."

Was there a next time? I don't know. It was crazy! We were completely unorganized. I remember one night we had twenty-four people show up at the same time for their first class. Twenty-four! I had to move the main class into another area and hold a special basic class for all these new people. I remember finishing that night and thinking, "This is it. This location will bring us to the next level." My mind was asking really positive, *what if* questions. "What if I could have a major impact on all of these people's lives? What if I can expand my brand nationwide and touch the lives of thousands of more students?"

With this influx of busyness, I was in over my head. I knew we were missing opportunities to connect and thought I probably should get better with that, but I was doing pretty well—or so I thought. In spite of myself, I began searching for a new business mentor—my first since leaving that coaching group three years previously.

As I was searching, we were approaching D-Day: the due date for the first rent payment at the new location. No problem! Now, if it wasn't clear before, let me clarify this for you: I disliked doing the numbers. Math, accounting, numbers tracking all made me want to scream into my pillow. I knew my strengths, and none of them involved numbers. But the approaching deadline forced my hand. Besides, we were finally holding our Grand Opening Party, and I had to plan for that, too. But I was naïve. Here's why.

In jiu-jitsu and all martial arts, there's always a chance that you outperform your belt level. For instance, you could be a blue belt in BJJ but achieve black belt proficiency in one move, like, say, a triangle choke from the guard position. That means if you're a blue belt, and you catch a black belt in a triangle choke, you could beat them. You might think you're pretty hot stuff at that point. You beat a black belt! But then the black belt will beat you the next fifty times, and she won't let her guard down for you to make that move again.

When I achieved black belt, I gained an awareness of how delusional I had been in this way. All the things I had *thought* I knew were nothing. I was, like, "Shit, I thought I was pretty good when I was a purple belt. Now I'm a black belt, and even though I know more, I'm humbler because I can see more. I can see things that I didn't know I needed to know." In other words, your martial arts horizon expands as you increase your knowledge.

This was that moment for me as an entrepreneur. I had thought I was a black belt in business, but in reality, I was only a blue belt at best.

When I looked at the numbers, I knew something was wrong. The revenue wasn't there. I crunched the numbers again. What was going on? We had all of these new students. Where was their tuition? Obviously we must have had some delinquencies or some students who temporarily froze their memberships. I called over Jeremy, who helped track those items for me.

"How many delinquencies do we have right now?"

"Um. Only a few, actually," he said.

I gulped. "How many frozen memberships?"

"About eight."

Crap. Those numbers were normal.

That's when I called up the student roster. Right before we had left the old location, we had 170 students. Here we were, almost six months later, and the active roster was at a whopping 173 students. In over five months, we had netted only three new enrollments. I wasn't running a school; I was operating a revolving door. All of a sudden my *what ifs* turned very dark. "What if we lose more students? What if we don't enroll more?"

All the marketing efforts were working—they were getting people to call and show up—but we had no systems to enroll and retain those people. I was as busy and productive as a hamster in a wheel. I had gotten effective at marketing, but I was only a blue belt level in every other area of my business. I needed help.

The Teacher Appears

I've heard the saying that the teacher appears when the student is ready. I was screwed, so the timing couldn't have been more perfect when Lloyd Irvin first put on a marketing seminar. Lloyd was an MMA and jiu-jitsu guy who ran an immensely successful school. He was renowned within the martial arts community not only for his business acumen but also for the achievements of his students in MMA and jiu-jitsu. Early on, some accused him of being a belt-giving sellout, but the results spoke for themselves.

The introductory event was only $97, as he was opening up his program to the public for the first time. Unlike the ill-fitting first coaching group, this guy knew a lot about the business side of martial arts.

I went with a friend, and we listened as Lloyd spent fourteen hours on stage. The event was so laid back that Lloyd showed up in a tank top and sweatpants. But there was nothing lacking in his information. Yes, he was selling something, but he offered a lot of great content and answered questions. He struck me as wanting to make sure those who walked out without signing up for his mastermind group still gained a lot of value from their time. I had rent due. What I was doing wasn't working, and that was the only thing I knew for certain. It was a no-brainer. I signed up, attended his training, and enrolled in his monthly mentoring group.

It didn't take me long to see results. One of the things I had learned was how to properly run an introductory lesson and then enroll the new students. When I got back from training, I had already lined up an introductory class for seven different people in one day. I used what I had learned, applied the information, and all seven enrolled. I was like, "Holy shit! This works!"

Lloyd's program taught me a lot about marketing to new students, the enrollment process, and multi-tiered training programs. It also taught me the importance of pinpointing the exact goals and needs of every new student. Some wanted to be UFC fighters like Andrew Craig. Others wanted to lose ten pounds, get strong, and learn some self-defense moves in the process. These are things we knew logically before, but the training program helped cement these concepts and gave the team and me the tools we needed to grow to the next level . . . and to be able to pay the rent.

It worked. Not only did we pay our rent, but our student roster almost doubled, going from 173 to over 300 in less than a year. I wasn't yet at a black belt level entrepreneurially speaking, but at least I was no longer deluding myself. There was still a lot to learn.

Maturation Process

Some days I wish success could be easier. That I could spend all my time doing the things I enjoy—training, fishing, teaching, and giving clinics—and avoiding all the things I dislike—staff schedules, marketing, budget forecasts, paying bills, and handling conflicts, both personal and professional, among other things.

Maybe you have a similar list. If all we could do was what we enjoy and are naturally good at, life would be a whole lot simpler. The fact is, life isn't this way. No matter what you're doing with your life, there are times when you either choose to do what you dislike or avoid it and miss the opportunity to grow, because growth comes from consciously deciding to do the hard things. And guess what? All the hard work makes the reward of success infinitely sweeter. The hours of work, trial and error, failure and recovery—it is why champions cry after they finally achieve victory. Because *easy* was never what they signed up for. Business is not easy, winning is not easy, life is not easy. But each of these deserves your best effort and will pay you back with interest in the end.

Also, growth takes time. Mat time. Time staring at numbers and admitting you're clueless as to how to fix the issues. And with growth comes growing pains: the pain of realizing you screwed up, you don't know what you don't know, and the willingness to keep leaning into the pain and fear.

With all the new enrollments and systems, the next year provided more good news. With guidance from Lloyd and his mastermind team, we finally upgraded our website to a modern look more in line with our brand's image and with a better contact form. In other news, my cousin, Andrew Craig, furthered his professional fighting career with wins in two International Extreme Fight Association (IXFA) competitions and one Legacy Fighting Championship (LFC) competition. In addition, he would soon make his mark in the UFC.

And yes, we had many bright, eager new faces. Some people might say to be quiet about growth because you'll look like you're selling out—as if we're a belt mill just handing out belts to underqualified students for the sake of collecting their dues. That's never been us and never will be. We train very hard. But that doesn't mean we don't have fun in the process.

Some days I lose, some days I win. Same for my coaches, staff, and students. As I write this, Cameron just came off a hard loss. That's okay. Losses are a part of life, too. He's already back in class working toward the next goal. I try to teach what I've learned: if you're winning, you don't stop and get comfortable there, and if you're losing, you don't sit still and stagnate. Never regret the effort you put into something just because you didn't get desired results. Effort is never wasted. Sure, I spent six months spinning my wheels and spending my time, but it wasn't wasted. It brought me to a lesson I desperately needed to learn.

Most of all, I learned to stop playing the spinning-hamster-wheel-in-your-head *what if* game. Yes, it can be positive. But when it's not grounded in reality, it can also be devastating. If you are just sitting there with your thoughts, you can either be delusionally happy, which is an inaccurate view of reality, or delusionally upset, which is equally inaccurate. Once in a while I will catch myself playing out these thoughts like, "What if we don't enroll anyone this way for several months? What if I have a fight with one of the other employees and fire them, and then what if . . ." It is not hard for a couple of negative things to come into your head and sidetrack you. It can pull you off your rhythm and almost make you want to sit still, immobilized.

But what's amazing is that as soon as I stop thinking *what if* and just start working, I start feeling better. I can't control every single business metric or every student that quits. I can't control every employee that does something in a way other than what I would like. However, I can control how I respond—that's the most important control of all.

Now, just because I was figuring out some things back in 2010 didn't mean everything was rainbows and butterflies going forward. The road to my visualized success was straightening and getting smoother, but there were still many dips along the way.

Enthusiasm is common. Endurance is rare.

—Angela Duckworth[16]

Do not think that what is hard for you to master is humanly impossible; and if it is humanly possible, consider it to be within your reach.

—Marcus Aurelius[17]

I hated jumping out of airplanes, I hated shooting guns, I hated the job as a Navy SEAL—but I did it because I wanted to change myself. Everything you do, I'm not really comfortable doing, but if you choose to go that route, to be a Navy SEAL, you might as well go be the hardest motherfucker in the world.

—David Goggins[18]

CHAPTER 8

Punches and Push-Ups

The road of life has many dips. It's like a roller coaster. If you're moving forward at all, you're going to experience highs and lows, twists and turns. I think the roller coaster gets crazier if you choose to become an entrepreneur. Imagine riding on the tracks with a pea-soup-thick fog a few feet in front of you. You can't see everything that's coming. The track bends a little and you can make a quick guess, but you go over the rise and find there's no track at all and you have to build it real quickly as you go. But if you get off the ride or plateau, it can feel a little depressing even if you're further ahead than you were. The good thing about this ride is that it doesn't go back to where you began—unless that's where you want to go.

---

16 Angela Duckworth, *Grit: The Power of Passion and Perseverance* (New York: Scribner, 2016), 58.
17 Quoted in Vivek Mather, *Cracking into Super Brains with 6000 Supreme Quotes* (New Delhi: Sudera, 2017), 117.
18 David Goggins, *Can't Hurt Me: Master Your Mind and Defy the Odds* (Lioncrest, 2018), 61.

Tony Robbins says, "When people succeed, they party. When people fail, they ponder. Rarely do you change your life at a party. But when you ponder, you come up with new distinctions and ideas to change your life." I had a lot more pondering left to do.

You've seen my ups and downs so far. I've struggled with cash flow, marketing, and enrolling students. It was literally a two-steps-forward, one-step-back journey for the most of it. However, one of the most trying times was yet to come—not in terms of financial loss, but in terms of making a mistake that almost destroyed my personal reputation and the credibility of my school.

But for a change, I had mostly ups for one season.

Success in the Octagon

While I always enjoy my own personal successes—who doesn't?—nothing beats watching my students grow and mature, not only in their jiu-jitsu mastery but also in their personal lives. Advertising that BJJ training helps self-esteem, courage, and confidence is more than just catchy sales copy; it's 110 percent true. Any time you dedicate yourself to pursuing something that challenges you both physically and mentally, forces you to break through your limiting beliefs, and makes you show up every day, you are going to improve in those three areas.

Remember Cameron from chapter 5? Fourteen years old, shy, and socially awkward when he joined in 2008? Despite his shyness, he held on to the growth mindset. He never gave up and became passionate about his jiu-jitsu training. As he moved up through the ranks, he eventually became an instructor in the kids' classes. Kids love him!

But by 2012, Cameron was ready to step up to yet another level. As a blue belt, Cameron decided he wanted to become a mixed martial arts (MMA) fighter. If you're not familiar with MMA, it goes beyond the grappling and groundwork of BJJ. To be successful, you need to have many other skills, including Muay Thai, boxing, and wrestling. This didn't faze Cameron. With the same gusto with which he approached everything he wanted, he jumped into the additional months of training to prepare for his first MMA fight.

The big night came on July 27, 2012. I sat ringside and cheered Cameron on as he battled the formidable Jose Ceja. I think I was more nervous prior to this match than any of my own tournament matches. The bell rang and they were off. Cameron threw the first punch but missed. Then Jose slung out some great hooks that Cameron blocked. Cameron had an advantage—if he could get Jose to the mat, he'd likely win easily—but Jose was smart enough to avoid takedowns. Fifteen seconds before the end of the first round, Cameron tackled Jose and was in a good position on top delivering body blows. Unfortunately, the round ended before he could get Jose into a lock.

Round two was a different story. Jose hit hard and fast with a close-body attack. Cameron, looking for space, pushed him off, and that's when Jose made his mistake: when he dropped his guard he was at the perfect distance from Cameron, who delivered a left leg kick that landed on the side of Jose's head with a crack like a tree snapping in half. Jose dropped like a sack of potatoes. It must have taken Cameron a few seconds of racing adrenaline to realize what had happened, because he charged in to finish the job before the referee waved him off. That's when you could see it hit him—he had won his first MMA fight. He raised his arms in triumph as the crowd cheered and celebrated the outstanding blow. I screamed so loud I think I went hoarse.

Had he lost, I still would've been proud of him for following his passion and working through all of his challenges both in jiu-jitsu and in life, but his winning in grand fashion only made my pride for him that much sweeter. It's more fun to celebrate than to console.

Earlier that same year, Andrew Craig got the big call. He was to be a last-minute replacement to fight Kyle Noke at UFC on FX2 in March. Andrew was undefeated at the time, having won fights in IXFA, Legacy (as mentioned), as well as the Bellator. Now he had the opportunity to show his work on the biggest MMA stage in the world. We packed our bags and headed out to Sydney, Australia, two weeks before the fight. Besides me, Andrew's coach from Austin, Robby Rabadi, also joined to be cageside during this fight.

According to Robby, he and I first met when we were both blue belts at a Dallas tournament. I have no memory of this. The first time *I* remember meeting him was back when he was a brown belt around 2009. At that time, he was already coaching MMA fighters, including my cousin Andrew in jiu-jitsu and Muay Thai. He had just started a school and teaching martial arts full time and wanted to continue advancing his own ju-jitsu training. So I began working with Robby and teaching him what I had learned about business while he grew his school in Austin. Robby and I hit it off because our personalities are so similar. Now, he has become one of my closest friends.

Going back to the story, Andrew got the call informing him that he was a replacement in the Australian tournament. The three of us flew to Australia. We stayed and trained in a hotel, getting Andrew ready for his big fight. In fact, we were training in the hotel's gym when we encountered another Seal. No, not a marine. Seal, the music artist and winner of four Grammys, was working out in the hotel gym. Andrew and I were finishing a workout when we noticed him, and meanwhile, Robby was leaning up against a pillar checking his messages on his phone. Seal had just finished his workout, so Andrew went up to him.

"Hey, would it be cool if my friends and I got a picture with you?" he asked.

"Yeah, man, sure," Seal said. "Just ask your friend not to film me while I'm working out." He must have thought Robby was taking pictures with his phone.

"No, of course not," Robby said, a little taken aback.

Seal wasn't satisfied with that answer. He looked right at Robby, all six foot four and 330 pounds of him and said, "Why did you answer first?"

Robby was flustered and didn't know how to respond. We went from thinking it was kind of cool that this famous guy was working out in the same room to being defensive because he was tearing into Robby for doing something he didn't do.

"I don't know what you're talking about," Robby finally said.

"Listen, man," Seal said, not letting up. "I've been in the business over twenty years. I've seen every trick in the book, and I don't appreciate it."

Robby's jaw dropped. Actually, all of our jaws dropped. We didn't quite know what to say.

We took the picture and Seal left. That's when Robby came to his senses. "Who the fuck does that guy think he is? Like I'd want to sneak a video of him working out!"

So to this day, we like to kid him about it. I never miss an opportunity to chide him a little. "Hey Robby, you need to step up in this situation, man. Don't back down like you did with Seal."

Oh, and in other news, Andrew did win the fight. It was quite the accomplishment and a solid notch in his belt to win at such a high level. He had flown across the globe and was now a winning UFC fighter.

Growth and Challenges

It almost always takes a while to find your groove when running a business. It's like being a chef: there are recipes and proven methods, but you have to find your own style and flavor. In 2013, I felt like I was finally finding my groove. The economy was rebounding, and we had grown with the help of Lloyd Irvin and his team's business coaching. The year brought consistency for a change and things were finally beginning to feel normal for the most part.

However, running the Spring location was getting more and more taxing as I divided my attention and coaches between the two locations. Serendipitously, I learned that my friend, student, and Team Tooke coach Jace Pitre hated his job in the oil fields. His employer would send him up to Oklahoma, the Dakotas, wherever they needed him. I began wondering if Jace would be interested in buying the Spring location. If ever I had a potential win-win situation, this was it. I'd be able to focus on my main location, and Jace would have the opportunity to teach a sport that he loves as much as I do. With a gentlemen's agreement, Jace purchased and took over the Team Tooke Spring location early that year.

Transferring the business title and assets into Jace's name was easy enough. The lease, on the other hand, was a bit sticky. I'd signed a transferrable lease with the landlord, but transferring it into Jace's name meant paying the landlord an $1,800 fee. I'd known Jace for eight years by this point and implicitly trusted him. We agreed that the lease and utilities would remain in my name and he would pay them directly. No fee, problem solved! Or so I thought.

Around the same time, controversy erupted around my mentor Lloyd Irvin's organization involving two of his students. Sadly, I had to leave his business group, but we remain on friendly terms to this day.

Despite losing the sounding board for all my ideas, we were able to keep going with what I had already learned. By this time, I'd learned enough to know that I needed to know more. But for now, I had to move forward without the guidance I'd come to rely on.

When summer rolled around, it became clear that Jace, who continued to train with me even though he was running his own location, had exceeded the requirements necessary for a black belt. Tying a new belt on a student is an experience that never gets old, and it's much sweeter when it's the highly sought-after black belt that represents years of dedication and relentless work. I tied Jace's on in August.

Turning Pro

The year 2013 was good for me in so many ways. Most memorable of all was my MMA debut fight. I was turning thirty-two and I guess I had a mild mid-life crisis—or maybe a one-third-life crisis. Though I never wanted to be a professional fighter, competing in at least one MMA fight had always been on my bucket list. I wasn't getting any younger, and I certainly wasn't going to wait until I was forty. With the decision made, I began the arduous training regimen months in advance.

As mentioned, it's called *mixed* martial arts for a reason. Fighters train in multiple styles. If I could get my opponent on the ground immediately I'd be all set, but my opponent would know that and do everything in his power to stop me from accomplishing that goal. While I'd trained off and on with UFC Fighters Andrew Craig and Yves Edwards, and I'd dabbled in multiple styles over the years, it was time to get serious about expanding my fighting repertoire and improving my striking skills.

The fight was set for November 1, and I began training. Besides running the school and continuously training in BJJ, I added Muay Thai for the boxing and kicking elements and became more proficient at wrestling for better takedowns. I knew that my opponent's strength was *striking*. All I had to do was get him to the ground, and I'd have the advantage. But I figured he knew this as well and would avoid takedowns at all costs. If I couldn't get him down, I'd better hold my own in the stand-up game. The problem is I never developed my punches too well. I could punch hard and fast, but I kept too much tension in my muscles, where a true boxer learns to stay loose. Another thing I didn't learn: not flinching, which is something they teach all strikers. If I flick my hands in front of your face, you're going to flinch. It's a natural human response. But when you flinch, you can't see what your opponent is doing. While you're flinching, he could blindside you with a follow-up combo and end the fight with a knockout.

Despite my shortcomings, I figured I was ready. It was only one fight after all.

I chose to fight in the always excellent Fury Fighting Championship. It's run by my student and friend Eric Garcia, but that's not why I chose it. It's just a damn good event, and Eric has had a ton of success with his efforts in fighting promotions.

The original plan was to fight as a lightweight amateur. Many black belts fight as an amateur their first time out, so I felt this would be best for my first go around. I typically weigh around 175 pounds, so I would just need to quickly cut twenty pounds to achieve the required weight of 155 pounds before the fight. That was the plan—except they couldn't find anyone to fight me as an amateur. Eventually, the only option was to fight as a welterweight professional. The target weight was 170 pounds. I'd only have to cut five pounds for weigh-in. My opponent, Rashid Abdullah, on the other hand, typically fought at 185 pounds, meaning he'd have to cut fifteen pounds to make weight.

October 31, 2013—weigh-in day. The weigh-in always happens the day before to give fighters time to rehydrate and recover before the fight. To make weight, all I had to do was drink a little less water and skip breakfast. Rashid walks in looking like a scarecrow, he'd lost so much weight. We stripped down to our undies and got on the scales. I weighed 170 pounds even. Rashid weighed 171 pounds. He was overweight by one pound. In this situation, I had the option to require him to make weight by the deadline a few hours away. I could have forced the issue and Rashid would have had to find a way to lose the pound in time. The idea is to make your opponent wear himself down before the fight. But I really didn't care.

"No, close enough. It's fine," I said. That might have been a mistake. We posed for the photos holding up our fists like we were about to go at it, and I thought that he looked so scrawny. *I can take this guy.*

Fight night arrived, and I was ecstatic. It was right here in Houston, and a bunch of my coaches and students were in attendance. Then I realized *everyone was there*, and I got nervous. I began thinking, "Oh, God. Everyone is watching. It would suck to be knocked out in five seconds, so hopefully that doesn't happen. Ideally, it'd be great to get him down, choke him out, and win quickly." My thoughts were racing from one unlikely scenario to the other.

My buddy Todd Moore was fighting that night, too. Since the time Todd and I started training together, he had become a great coach at Team Tooke and was teaching kids fundamentals and adult kickboxing. But he always kept up his own training and competition goals. Fortunately for me, his fight was first. Todd had been fighting in the MMA arena for years by then and had established himself as one of the top MMA fighters to ever come out of Houston. He won his fight quickly. A rear naked choke ended his opponent before the end of the first round. It was a confidence booster for me. I remember thinking, "Okay, we got one!"

A few fights later, it was my turn.

I went out, I was feeling pumped, and the crowd was cheering and shouting my name. I stepped into the hexagonal cage and my entry door locked behind me. Then Rashid stepped into the ring.

Rashid had ballooned up to his full weight. It was around this moment I thought, "Holy crap, what have I gotten myself in to?" It's in moments like these that you question the sanity behind your original decision.

Some fighters use IVs to rehydrate quickly after making weight. Rashid must have used every IV bag available. He was huge! Already taller than me by three inches with longer legs and arms, he now had a lot more muscle than he'd had the day before. Rashid was bigger, stronger, and meaner. Hydration is an amazing thing.

So now I was locked in a cage with a man that wanted to beat me until either I gave up or they had to pry him off me because I could no longer defend myself. It was too late to turn back now.

The ref checked in with us as we faced off, and then the bell rang. I just started shooting nervous kicks at his legs as hard as I could. He didn't defend the low attack, and I exploited it. I got him pretty good three times that first round. Three minutes doesn't sound like a long time, but when you're in the cage trying to survive, you begin to wonder if time has stopped. I did the best I could, got my kicks in, and had gotten him to react to jabs and fakes. I saw an opportunity and shot for his legs. I dove in with all I had and got him on the ground moving into a good mounted position. "This is it! I got him where I want him." Ding, ding, ding! End of round one.

Damn. I got my mount, but it was too late in the round. This was going to be a long bout.

Round two. Same as the first with the kicks and dancing around, except Rashid connected hard—one good punch, a cross followed by a glancing right hook, that pushed me back against the chain links. I had to wiggle out or he was going to pummel me. Two minutes and twenty seconds in, I shot for his legs again. Oh, boy, this time I got him. I wrapped him up and he was wiggling around. All I had to do was work in and get him into a lock. Bell rang. End of round two.

Double damn.

By this time I wasn't feeling so great. My lip was busted and my eye was swelling up after his one-two combo. I didn't know who was winning. I remember Andrew looking me in the eye and saying, "All right, time to stop fucking around! Get the takedown earlier and get the fight where you want it!" I wish.

In round three, I went back to what was working—kicking his legs as fast and as hard as I could and avoiding letting my guard down. He managed to grab my leg when I kicked a couple of times and had me off balance, but I wriggled free. I tried to get an early takedown, but he was ready for it.

A few people asked me later, "You're a black belt in jiu-jitsu. Why didn't you just take him down?" Well, it's not that easy to take an athlete down, especially a trained fighter who is bigger and stronger than you are.

In the final minute of the fight, we ended up rolling around on the mat—him avoiding my attacks, and me avoiding his punches. When the final bell rang, I wasn't sure about my chances.

We stood in the middle of the cage, the ref between us, awaiting the verdict. I won the first judge's decision. Yay! Rashid won the second. It all came down to the final judge. Win or lose, I'd done the best I could and had finally fought professionally. I had no regrets. The announcer continued, "In the final round . . . the winner by split decision . . ."—I held my breath and hopefully pumped my fist in the air—"Travis Tooke!"

I did it? I did it!

I raised my fists in the air and hugged the bear I just battled. Afterward, talking to my team, I told them that I felt like I had gotten some favoritism from the local judges. Maybe I shouldn't have won—I did have a swollen lip and a black eye—but he was limping out of the venue.

"No, Travis, you definitely won!" Todd told me.

Later I had the chance to watch the video Todd took. He and the judges were right. It was close—very close—but I had won my first and only MMA fight. One more item off the bucket list.

Now remember, my cousin Andrew is a UFC fighter—a pretty good one, with an undefeated amateur record and a pro record of nine wins and four losses. When we get together at family gatherings, I always acknowledge his fighting prowess and quickly add, "But remember, there's only one undefeated fighter in this family."

The Fall of Spring

As 2013 drew to a close, not all was well. The Spring location was doing okay under Jace's leadership. Jace is a gifted teacher with a charismatic style that the students love. When we agreed to the sale, it seemed like the perfect fit. It turned out he didn't like the other side of the martial arts business—the structured organization, marketing, and daily operations. This is true for many business owners who get into business because they love what they do. There's a great example in Michael Gerber's *The E-Myth*: Sarah loves making pies so she opens a pie shop. As an entrepreneur, though, Sarah soon finds herself doing everything *except* making pies.

Jace's situation was just like fictional Sarah's. Jace loves teaching. If given the choice between budgeting for and planning the next quarter's marketing campaign or giving a private, two-hour lesson, he'd always opt for the latter. It didn't take him long to realize that operating business this way was not sustainable for a lifelong career.

One day near the end of the year, Jace called me and said he wanted to meet me for a half hour. I didn't ask why and agreed. We met up along with a student of Jace's named James.

"So, I'm pretty much done with the business thing," Jace said when we met. "I love teaching, but that's all I love."

I nodded. I had the sense that this was where he was headed, and I began to wonder what the next step would be; Jace already had a solution.

"James has been training with me for a while now," he continued. "He's a good teacher, and he's got a lot of business experience. He's interested in buying the school—with your blessing, of course, since it's still going to be a Team Tooke location."

After thinking it over, I decided to approve. I'd met James once before and spoke with him quite a bit that day. He seemed like a stand-up guy. I trusted Jace's judgment, and the move helped Jace out of a difficult situation. On top of that, this sale allowed us to keep a second school. Problem solved.

Jace made a similar agreement with James to the one that we had made. A handshake sealed the arrangement, and Team Tooke Spring was now in James's capable hands. Or so I thought.

A few months later, in the spring of 2014, I started hearing bad reports and getting calls from disgruntled students. They alleged that James had misrepresented membership agreements and had taken their money under false pretenses. I've always run my business with a high level of honesty and integrity, so these reports did not sit well with me. I gave him the benefit of the doubt in the beginning, assuming he was just having some trouble adjusting. He would insist that these were all just misunderstandings, but they persisted. Eventually, they became a real problem. I needed to have a talk with James.

I got him on the phone and laid it out quickly. "James, you can't be using the Team Tooke name anymore. I know you're figuring things out, but I can't have all these issues and complaints associated with our name."

He got a little defensive about the allegations, and I listened, but in the end he understood. We took the Spring location off of our website and promotional materials. I felt a little sad. It was our first attempt at franchising, and it ended in failure. I was sure that I'd learn my lessons and be ready for the next time. This chapter of my business was over . . . for now.

Fit as a SEAL

Though I was more than happy with my path in life, I still find a part of me that wonders what my life might have been like had I been able to enlist in the Navy. If that pesky one-time eczema thing on my finger hadn't happened, would I have passed Basic Underwater and Demolition/SEAL (BUD/S) training? The program has a notoriously high failure rate of over 80 percent.

It's a question that pops up whenever we have a SEAL train with us, and there have been a few, including *Lone Survivor* author Marcus Luttrell. Unlike the Hollywood image, most SEALs are pretty easygoing guys who are just passionate soldiers and who remain physically and mentally ready for just about any challenge. Would I have made it? Maybe I had a chance to find out.

While reading a book, I came across the name Mark Divine. Mark is a former SEAL commander who has authored books about leadership and mental toughness. I visited Mark's website, and as I was looking around, I saw that he runs a program called SEALFIT, a five-day training event modeled after the SEAL Hell Week. If you're unfamiliar with Hell Week, it's the fourth week of BUD/S training that involves four days and five nights of testing and training on a maximum of four hours sleep. It isn't called *Hell* Week for nothing. The program on his site was a condensed version for civilians, which meant many of the physical challenges but none of the weapons or combat training. Maybe it was my teenage dream stirring within me, but I got excited when I saw the word *SEAL* everywhere, with pictures of men and women training on the beach. Later on I found myself frequently thinking about the SEALFIT program. It wasn't cheap, and that kept me from saying yes right away. But it continued to bug me, until one day I thought, "Screw it. I'm never going to do this if I don't just do it." So I signed up, paid the fee, and then said, "Shit. Now I have to do it." I'm good at tricking myself into commitment.

SEALFIT sent me a list of the gear I had to pack, and I got to work buying what I needed for my journey to "Hell." I bought everything on the list: a pair of combat boots, tennis shoes, six white t-shirts with my name stenciled on the front, workout shorts, six pairs of hiking socks, three pairs of military combat utility pants, goggles (I upgraded to the official SEALFIT dive mask), and swim trunks.

Weeks later, I was at the airport waiting for a plane to San Diego, which is just south of Encinitas, California, where the facility is. The problem was I was booked on an overbooked standby flight and ended up on another flight to a layover city before arriving in Los Angeles. Now I had to rent a car, make the hour-and-a-half drive down the coast, drop the rental off, and get a cab. I ended up being an hour late for the Sunday evening kickoff. Not a great start. At least it was only check-in day.

One of the coaches there got me started. Though my team was already out on a run, he set up a personal warm-up routine for me. I wish I had made it in time for the run; my workout was way harder. I did ten bag cleans (lifting a weighted bag with handles), ten box jumps, ten burpees, and a quarter-mile run—ten rounds of all four exercises!

By the time I finished, my team had made it back in from their run. There were twelve of us in this mixed-age group, which included guys in their late teens and early twenties, business owners, and a dentist. I was in the middle at thirty-three years old. After introductions, we went to the barracks—two rooms with three bunk beds each. I imagined this was what summer camp was like, except we wouldn't be holding hands and singing "Kum Ba Yah" by a warm fire.

Each day we were up at five a.m. and in bed at eleven p.m. A better schedule than real SEAL training, but we were still exhausted at the end of each day, and six hours sleep didn't feel like nearly enough.

The first day involved the physical fitness test. Anyone who failed was sent packing. But first, the leaders had to address a couple of lame guys who had no idea how to stencil their names onto those six white t-shirts. I was one of them. I had scrawled "Tooke" in free-hand, block print. Those of us who failed this basic instruction had to do it over again properly.

After a healthy, specially prepared organic breakfast (all meals were very healthy), we had to prove we were able to handle the week ahead. To pass the fitness test, I had to do fifty push-ups in two minutes, fifty sit-ups in two minutes, fifty air squats in two minutes, ten dead-hang pull-ups, and a one-mile run in combat boots and utility pants in less than nine minutes and thirty seconds. In addition, I had to do one Murph in less than seventy-five minutes.

A Murph is named after Navy Lieutenant and SEAL Michael P. "Murph" Murphy, a Medal of Honor recipient. Murph was killed in action in Afghanistan in 2005 after standing in the line of fire in order to have a clear radio signal to communicate his team's position and dire situation. He willingly sacrificed himself to save the rest of his team.

A Murph consists of a one-mile run, one hundred pull-ups, two hundred push-ups, three hundred air squats, and a second one-mile run. I'd paid good money to be tortured.

As tough as day one was, it was actually the easiest of them all. The following four days were grueling. Every morning we lined up in formation. This was followed by push-ups or holding a plank position. The longest plank position hold was twenty-nine minutes long. That super sucked! Beside our various workouts, we would have one or two classes a day where we learned about goals, mindset, breathing techniques, and mental toughness. Then we'd go get punished—I mean pumped—again. We pushed sleds, swam lengths in the pool, squatted, crunched, crawled, carried, and probably cried.

The facility was only a block or two from the beach, so we'd be there quite a bit. We carried a giant log as a team, did curls with it, ran with it, and carried it on our shoulders. We ran maneuvers as two-man teams where one of us was "dead" and the others had to carry him, and then we'd switch. We sat in the cold Pacific Ocean, backs to the horizon, with our arms interlocked as waves crashed over us, so we felt like we were going to drown.

Probably my favorite beach drill was the Sugar Cookie. It had nothing to do with baking. Though I did well in all the drills, I wasn't the best guy at any drill except for this one, because I found it really fun. I learned that a painful task can be bearable if you look for the element of fun in it.

Now, a Sugar Cookie is when you run out into the cold ocean water and completely submerge yourself before returning to the shore to cover yourself from head to toe in sand. I was the fastest every time, and when I won for the third time in a row, I was allowed to sit out the next round while everyone else had to do the drill again. This was known as "It pays to be a winner." But as my teammates ran off, I asked the coach, "Can I do it again?"

The coach smiled and said, "Go for it, Tooke!"

I guess I was having too much fun.

The hardest night was Wednesday (technically, Thursday morning around midnight). We had heard from former participants that at some point they were likely going to wake us up in the middle of the night, and we suspected it might be that night. We were right. It didn't matter how prepared we were . . . it was fucking miserable.

This nightmarish alarm blared while we were sleeping, and the leaders yelled at us to get out of bed. Of our team's two rooms, one was told to get dressed in pants and boots, and the other was told to wear tennis shoes and shorts. When we got down to the training area, everyone was dressed differently. I was in the "wrong" group. They told us it was our fault, and we all had to go change. I learned later that they did this on purpose.

When we came back, we all had to hold a push-up position while they sprayed us with water. Then they dragged out a big 150-gallon plastic tub filled with several bags of ice and water. They picked me first. "Tooke! Bear-walk over to that tub and get in without spilling a drop!" A bear walk is almost like walking in the downward dog yoga position. I had to walk on all fours with my butt in the air and every limb fairly straight, and then I had to enter the tub headfirst and come out from underneath a bar they had strategically placed right in the center. So there was no chance to get used to the cold. Then I had to sit in the ice-cold water. As my breathing raced—you know, because I was freezing to death—the coaches talked me through it. "Breath slowly, deep breaths, control yourself. You got this." This was actually comforting.

Once I got my breathing under control, the coach said, "Okay, Tooke, talk me through, step-by-step, one of the first moves that you teach a new student on their first day of jiu-jitsu class." (The coaches knew what each of us did back home.)

My brain raced around trying to pick a basic technique while working to control my breathing and endure the pain of the ice water, which was being stirred with a canoe paddle to make it feel colder—kind of like sitting in a moving stream. I finally thought of a technique. I picked the move: Escape from the Mount. With chattering teeth and short, panting breaths, I recited the instructions.

The coach said, "Good job, Tooke. Good job. Now step out of the tub and get back into push-up position with your teammates. And do not spill any water."

Following our ice baths, lots of push-ups, and more water sprayed in our faces, we headed out to the beach. It was around one a.m., and it was time for some war games. This part was super fun. Our team of six was told that the enemy, the other team, would be near us in fifteen minutes. We had to bury ourselves in sand and hide. Luckily enough, they picked me as the leader of this operation. I immediately shouted, "Dig!" and we all started digging in a panic. We had to bury ourselves and our backpacks under the sand right under a streetlight, which made everything easy to see.

The team found us easily, and we completely failed the mission. The lesson the coach taught us afterward was very valuable. He said, "No one took the time to breathe and assess the situation. You all panicked.

Even in panic situations, you almost always have time to take a breath, collect your thoughts, and make a better decision." Lesson learned.

When it was our turn to find the other team, they were well-hidden in the dark and spread apart. We found only three of them before time ran out. We continued to play a few more war games involving races and crawling in the sand, but the absolute hardest part was carrying a log with a teammate for a few hundred yards or more down the steps to the beach, back up the steps, and all the way back to headquarters. The weight wasn't too bad, but the log grinding on my shoulders was killing me. I kept having to switch sides, which didn't make my partner happy. He had tougher shoulders, I guess.

Around three a.m. we finally made it back to base, where we all had to lie down in a straight line, head to toe. As the coach gave us a chat about teamwork, they poured the ice tub on the ground and the water flowed under and around us. So we got to take another ice bath!

We got cleaned up and were allowed two hours' sleep before waking up and starting the next day, which came far too quickly.

On the final day, we did open-water swimming. Before we began, Mark Divine, the head coach and CEO of SEALFIT, gave us some advice. He said, "Does everyone have their knives with them in case of sharks?" We all looked around with confused smiles on our faces. "Remember, if you encounter a shark, the best thing to do"—he paused and eyed everyone on our team to make sure he had our full attention—"is to stab your swim buddy and swim like hell to shore."

We laughed in a sort of frail and terrified manner. The truth was that great whites did frequent those waters, so it wasn't entirely impossible to encounter one, just unlikely. The mission was simple: with our goggles and fins, we had to swim out past the waves and then swim against the current for about half a mile with a teammate. This is where I regretted buying the SEALFIT mask instead of goggles. It would have been great for scuba diving, but hard for swimming against the current; having my nose uncovered would have been better so I could breathe. I felt like I was drowning the entire time and slowed my teammate down because I had to turn to swim with my face up several times. The coaches were out there offering help, which was great. If a shark had wanted to get me, I would have been an easy meal.

When the swim was over, we felt exhausted but accomplished. Going through something like that together creates strong connections even with people whom you may not have much in common with. It's not unlike training with teammates in jiu-jitsu. Hard times make for strong bonds.

Breathe Like a Warrior

The final piece to the whole week seemed a little out of step with everything else we had accomplished. I'd gotten sand everywhere, I felt sore in muscles I'd forgotten I had, and I'd been nearly drowned at least three times. We had a few breaks for yoga, which was great as I was a longtime practitioner by this time on account of my herniated disc. All of that was awesome, but this last thing—breathing meditation? Really? We had done a few sets of five-minute box-breathing exercises during the week, but this was going to be for a full hour or so.

One of the coaches-in-training was a former soldier who had lost his leg from the knee down. I didn't even know he was wearing a prosthetic until he put his shorts on—he moved *that* fluidly. When he saw that the meditation was next, he got excited. "This is the best part!" he said, having been through SEALFIT a few times before.

Meditation was unexpected. A badass soldier getting excited about it was even more so. "What do you mean?" I asked.

"The last time I did it I was full-on-tears crying, it was so good."

This guy looked about as tough as anyone there. Him crying? No way.

We all funneled into a studio and had a seat on the floor, and this coach came in. Now this guy I'll refer to as the Hippie SEAL. He had these really relaxed baggy pants on, but at the same time had a tough-looking beard and tank top and gave off a weird, yet interesting vibe. He didn't look very nice, and he spoke with this strong, country-boy Texas accent. But looks can be deceiving. Hippie was nice—firm and tough, but nice.

"Everyone, lie on your backs," he instructed us.

Some intense instrumental music came on, and he walked us through an exercise for forty-five minutes. Using diaphragmatic breathing, we took sharp, intense inhales followed by rapid exhales. Then we'd hold our breath for as long as we could and relax our bodies. On and on, intense deep breathing, music, and focusing on sensations and emotions.

Then Hippie asks us probing questions like "What is truly important to you?" and "Who do you really love? Who are some people that you are maybe not on good terms with? What negativity do you need to let go of?"

I know what you're thinking. What kind of weird voodoo are they doing to get people ready for the military? It is hard to describe the experience. If I had heard somebody talk about it the way I am talking now, I'd have thought it sounded hokey and assumed these people were on drugs. But it's nothing like that.

Hippie kept giving us these trigger questions, and I was having thoughts, but they were incredibly focused. I saw these memories from my past—I saw people, I saw really bad arguments I'd had, and I saw really loving moments. Everything became clear. I narrowed down what was important to me to a few things, and then I realized I had this big pile of bullshit over here on the side that I had been wasting a lot of energy on. I got total clarity.

At the end, just like the soldier had said, about three quarters of us had tears streaming down our faces. Hippie then asked, "Does anyone feel like sharing?"

Now, before I go any further, I have to tell you that I have not always been one to share my feelings. Ingrid will attest to the fact that me and feelings seem to live on opposite sides of the city. Yet here I was surrounded by these tough guys—business leaders, young soldiers prepping for BUD/S, one guy who was going to Ranger School—and I shared what I was feeling without any hesitation. Because it was okay. I looked around at these "tough" guys and realized we had all just shared an incredible experience. And when I spoke, emotions poured out of me. It was like they were ripped from me.

SEALFIT was life-changing. And, no, they don't compensate me for sharing this story. It wasn't much fun until it was done, but when it was done, I'd been stretched beyond what I thought possible, and there was no way I was going back to who I was before. Little did I know that it prepared me to handle only months later the biggest betrayal of my trust I'd ever experienced.

*Your potential, the absolute best you're capable of—
that's the metric to measure yourself against. Your
standards are. Winning is not enough. People can
get lucky and win. People can be assholes and win.
Anyone can win. But not everyone is the best possible
version of themselves.*

—Ryan Holiday[19]

CHAPTER 9

Obsessions and Opportunities

Obsession sometimes gets a bad rap. It's often associated with addictions like gambling, drugs, and workaholism. Sometimes it's negatively ascribed to someone who is overly enthusiastic about one pursuit to the exclusion of everything else in life: "Man, he's obsessed!" I agree that an obsession can be a harmful, negative, even ruinous thing.

But done right, it can be a good thing—powerful, transformational, even magical.

I am obsessed with jiu-jitsu. And while many of my students span the spectrum of obsession from mild interest in physical and mental development to earning a black belt for the achievement itself, a handful are as obsessed as I am.

Here's what can make obsession something powerfully positive: combine it with passion, love, and the desire to grow. That's a winning formula. Obsession without any of these three ingredients can lead to a downward, myopic spiral. But when it's balanced with a sense of pursuing self-growth and love and support for others, obsession turns into real-world magic.

---

19 Ryan Holiday, *Ego Is the Enemy* (New York: Portfolio, 2016), 197.

I started with very little. Meager beginnings can lead to meager end-ings, but I think there are huge advantages to starting with very little. Once I found my path—jiu-jitsu—I became driven to do more with it and achieve something because I didn't have much to lose. Every time I achieved something I wanted—my black belt, my school, a student's success—I was driven to go deeper with jiu-jitsu, grow my business big-ger, and have even more impact on my students' lives. If I was given everything I needed from the beginning, I'm not sure I would have had enough drive—that undefinable spark—to succeed. If I had more than enough money, easy accessibility to BJJ professors, a solid business edu-cation, perhaps I would have made fewer big moves for fear of losing it all. Instead, by starting with very little, I found a strong reason to grow into the person I needed to be to become successful. And I'm still growing.

Through my obsession, passion, love for the sport and people, and desire to grow, I became competitive with myself. In fact, I learned that being more competitive with myself than with others is the key. Beating someone as a way to gauge progress is fine (competition, money, etc.), but beating them for the sake of winning—meaning they lose—is selling yourself short. Your heart is in the wrong place, and focusing on beating someone at anything can become a destructive sort of obsession.

I've never been especially religious. I have, however, developed a strong sense of faith—faith in the martial arts path. For me, this jiu-jitsu obses-sion isn't a religious experience; it's a lifestyle. Jiu-jitsu has helped shape all the choices I've made as an adult: my career, my friendships, my de-cisions regarding nutrition and exercise. This path—this martial arts lifestyle—has never betrayed me. It has never let me down. I've had sit-uations with people in jiu-jitsu where things didn't work out. Those were painful, but it was never because of the path. It's just the nature of people and relationships. Unlike relationship issues, jiu-jitsu is not a problem to be solved. Like life, it is meant to be explored, enjoyed, ex-perienced, and improved upon.

My positive obsession continues to today. That drive hasn't gone away, because I'm still learning and growing. But once in a while I've grown complacent and lazy, and it has cost me.

Jiu-jitsu has never betrayed me. But people have.

Martial Con Artist

SEALFIT was a fun and forever memorable conclusion to 2014. Other than the blemish of having to tell James, the new owner of the Spring location, that he could no longer use the Team Tooke name and logo, the year was pretty good, all things considered. Besides, the Team Tooke MMA in Cypress was still going strong under the leadership of my friend Miguel Castro. We were growing again with my new mentor—more on him in a bit—and James was just another setback to be forgotten.

Only James wouldn't go away as quietly as I'd hoped.

It was early 2015 when I heard the rumor that James was opening another location. *Good for him!* I thought. *He must be doing pretty great now.* On a whim, I decided to call the Spring location landlord's office to check in on everything. You might remember that my name was still on the lease because I never transferred the lease over to James's name—Jace sold him the business, but the lease and the utilities were still in my name in order to avoid the hassle and the $1,800.

A woman answered the phone, and after brief greetings, I got down to business. "So everything must be good?"

She sighed—never a good sign. "Ah, no."

"No? What's going on?"

"James is over $20,000 behind on the rent."

Ouch. The lease was still in my name, meaning legally I was more than $20,000 behind on the rent. For some reason, I'd still not learned that crucial lesson: get all agreements in writing, even among friends.

The rent was $6,200 a month. "He's behind three months?!" I asked.

"No. Worse. He said he needed some time to catch up. He's only been paying half for the past six months. Then he stopped altogether this month. By the time the lease ends in a couple more months, it will be around $31,000."

Not good. I could feel my face flush and my ears tingling. I lashed out. "Why didn't you tell me? My name is on the lease, I should have known." I was mad at her for not telling me, but really she was just a convenient outlet for the emotions flooding through me. She didn't create this situation. I was shooting the proverbial messenger.

To her credit, she responded professionally—more professionally than I was able to be in that moment. "It didn't occur to me. I was used to dealing with James."

It became apparent that there was nothing she could do, and I realized that I had no legal leg to stand on. I had signed a paper that said I, Travis Tooke, being of not-so-sound mind (apparently) guaranteed that I would pay this money no matter what, even if this business sells twice.

Later that day, I got a call back from the head property manager. "I'm sorry, Travis, I thought she would have told you," he said.

"Well, she didn't."

He was courteous and apologetic, explaining that she was young and still learning the ropes; and while I appreciated the apology, it did nothing to quell my anger at the situation but especially at James. Six months of half-payments had gone by, and I hadn't even gotten a text message from the landlord's office saying, "Hey, there's a problem with rent."

I have no issue paying rent I owe on space I use to earn a living. But I was earning zero from James's business. He was apparently not making too much either. After sniffing around on some of the negative reviews online, it seemed that people complained that after they had cancelled their memberships, he was still charging their credit cards every month. Others prepaid and quit early because of his actions, but he wasn't refunding the unused portion of their payments. The amounts they claimed to have paid, however, didn't make sense. When I did the math, it averaged out to about twenty-one dollars a month per student. That wouldn't cover James's basic expenses even if he maxed out his enrollments. So much for him being a business wizard. Not that I was looking too hot myself at that moment.

My heart sank. $20,000 is a lot of money, especially when you're getting nothing in return. Jace needed to know what was happening. After all, he's the one who sold the business to James and vouched for him. But in the end, it was my own mistake in not transferring the lease that had got me to this point.

After ending the call with the landlord, I called Jace to break the bad news.

"Oh my God! What are we going to do?" Jace was shocked. I could hear panic in his voice. "This guy is screwing us. He doesn't even care. I don't think we can even talk to him he's so crazy." I wasn't expecting this reaction. After all, Jace had vouched for him, but I later learned that James hadn't kept faithful to their agreement. James had put a certain amount down when he bought the school and made his monthly payments until he stopped a number of months before. He still owed Jace quite a bit of money. When I learned that, I thought, *Okay, this is not a good person we're dealing with. He's not honoring any of his commitments.*

Well, I wasn't thinking in such harsh terms before I called Jace, but now I was beginning to panic, too. How were we going to get this guy to pay? Was he really crazy? I wasn't qualified to make that assessment. I'd only met him a few times, and he seemed like a decent guy. All I knew at this point was that he was a dishonest and incompetent business owner.

In the heat of the moment, we put our heads together and came up with a brilliant plan. James was moving his school—because he was being evicted—but still had all his gear inside: pro-shop gear, signage, and the expensive mats. We were going to force him to pay up by holding everything hostage. Did I say it was a brilliant plan? I meant juvenile and stupid.

I told Ingrid what was going on. "I'm going to take care of that guy!" I said as I explained my plan.

"Um, that's a bad idea. It's dangerous and probably illegal."

"Nah, it'll be fine. Watch."

Jace and I went to the school late that night. I still had a key; James had never changed the locks. We took his stuff and hid it so it was out of sight from the door and hired a locksmith to change the locks. My belief was that, since I was an unofficial landlord by proxy, the best way for me to make sure I got my money was to lock him out of his own school. It turned out this wasn't exactly legal.

Later that morning my phone rang. It was James. "Do you know anything about this?" he asked.

"Yeah, you're twenty grand behind on rent, and it's all on me. You're putting me in a very bad position. We're not going to let you move your stuff to your new place until you make this right."

James went ballistic. "You have no right to steal my stuff!"

I had to wait for him to stop swearing. "I didn't steal your stuff. Everything's there. The mats are up in the loft. Just pay your bill."

James calmed a little and told me that he was going to pay and make it right; he just got a little behind. I didn't relent. I wasn't unlocking those doors until the landlord got his money.

It didn't work.

First, James called another locksmith and had him pick the locks and then change them again later that day. I guess the locksmith didn't care whose name was on a lease as long as somebody was paying him. Next, I started seeing James's posts on social media about how "some punks" broke into his school and trashed the place. Even though he didn't name Jace and me, he used the hashtags "#ftt" and "#fuckteamtooke."

We'd done zero damage. We hid his stuff. The walls, signs, posters, floors, mats were all the same as we found them. We acted immaturely, sure, but we weren't thugs. And the funny thing about his posts is that, even though I had told him not to use my school's name a year before this, he had continued to advertise that he was a Team Tooke school this entire time. So in a way he was attacking himself in these "#ftt" posts.

Though I had acted rashly, I'm glad to say I didn't engage in his trolling and passive-aggressive social media attacks. But I was still livid that he was painting us as the bad guys when he was the one ripping off people. As I dove deeper, it got worse. Some people he had swindled were giving bad reviews online and on the Better Business Bureau's website. Every single one said "Team Tooke Spring." I'd spent the last eight years establishing my solid reputation both in business and teaching, and James was tearing it down within weeks. I'd never felt so overcome by anger, fear, and betrayal.

A day or so after the lockout, I was researching the law to see if there was anything else I could do. My anger and betrayal gave way to anxiety. I went pale as I read the text on a landlord legal advice website about how illegal it was to lock out a tenant before you take him to court. "This is bad," I thought. "Ingrid was right—again." Her rational mentality complements my quick reactions. Unfortunately, I didn't heed her warning.

I called Jace. His tone changed. Before, he had cursed the day James was born. Now he was worried about going to jail. So was I. Remember the *what if* question loop? I was stuck in a negative spiral. "What if I'm arrested? What if I'm teaching a kids' class with all the parents watching, and cops come in and arrest me?"

It wasn't going to jail that scared me. If I went to jail, I'd survive. I'd find a good lawyer who would prove that I was acting in ignorance with no harmful intent. I'd likely pay a fine and be done with it. That wasn't the issue. It was the mental movie I played where I got carted away in handcuffs in front of the parents with them assuming that I was a pedophile or something. People trashing my school's name online was one thing, but being misidentified—even for only a day or two—as a criminal would be a whole other issue. It didn't help that I spotted a police cruiser parked near the school when I arrived one morning. "Shit. Today's the day." Fortunately, it was just my paranoia, and he wasn't there for my sake.

But a couple of days later I did receive a phone call. "This is Officer Rogers with HPD. I'm calling about a reported incident." He went on to describe the lockout.

Uh-oh. "Yes, I changed the locks. But I have a key. The lease is in my name. I had a right to do that." Of course, I wasn't so sure, but I took a strong defensive position—maybe I was trying a little verbal jiu-jitsu.

"I'm not so sure about that. Do you have a written lease agreement with James?"

What? "No. But like I said—"

"Regardless. Whether or not you have an agreement, he could be considered your legal tenant as viewed by the law, which means he has rights that you violated."

Something smelled fishy about this cop. I don't doubt that he was a cop, but I'd read somewhere that cops weren't supposed to interpret law, only enforce it.

"Wait a minute," I said. "First of all, you're a police officer, and you don't necessarily know the law about this. But neither do I. I don't really want to talk to you about this. I'm done." Click.

I'm a law-abiding citizen—except for the street signs I keep putting up—and I was pretty sure I was right, but I didn't feel so good about telling a cop to go shove it, even if I was polite.

Then a report of that call showed up on social media—James's version.

"The officer asked him questions, but he was too cowardly to answer them," he wrote. There were probably more hashtags, if I remember right. But the post seemed to confirm my suspicions about that cop. How would James know the details of a private phone call? It doesn't seem like the sort of thing an investigating officer would share.

Things didn't get much better. Despite the promises James made to make good in a "few days," he didn't. I called him about a week later to see how the payments were going.

"Good. I just dropped off a check for $2,000 at the landlord's office this morning," James said.

"Really?"

"Yup."

What he didn't know is that I had already called the landlord and had him on hold on the other line. "Hold on a minute," I said, and then transferred to line two. "He says he dropped off two grand this morning."

"What?! We haven't seen him in weeks."

So that's how it was going to be. First ripping off customers, and now lies. I was shaking I was so furious. I think I had been in denial about James, but now the situation grew clear: he had no intention of paying back the arrears. The landlord had no option but to lock him out. Except they did it the right way.

That didn't stop James, though. He took all of his stuff and moved to his new location. That part of the rumors was true. He *was* opening another school to ditch the landlords of the first one. And it was literally right across the street, in another plaza directly across four lanes of traffic and a median.

The old landlord called me and said, "I'm sorry, but your name's on the lease. You will owe the full $31,000 to finish out the lease term."

I told him I'd call him back. It wasn't my fault James didn't pay the guy, but I took full responsibility for not signing an agreement with James or having the lease transferred. There was no one to blame for that but me. I called Jace and told him about how much was owed.

Jace felt badly about the whole ordeal. I didn't blame him for trusting James, though. James was a charismatic guy; he was the one who did these awful things. Despite that fact, Jace made me a promise. "I'll pay you back—every penny—but money's tight right now. There's no way I can pay you the full amount."

"Let's see if it has to be the full amount," I said.

I called the landlord back and told him I didn't have $31,000 in cash. It was true, I didn't. But I could pay him $15,000 if we ended this today. He quickly agreed. A little too quickly, actually, and I remember thinking, "Dammit, I should have offered $10,000." Oh well.

With the landlord satisfied, he opened the doors for us so we could take anything James had left behind. There wasn't much, but he did leave a big red channel letter sign—those signs with 3D lettering—that said "Mixed Martial Arts." My brother JP and I were there loading it into the back of my truck when we noticed James across the street at his new school talking to the new landlord outside. I saw him look over at us for a moment, so we held the sign high above our heads for a second as if to say, "Last week you said you'd have us arrested. Look what we're doing now." Immature? Yes. Satisfying? Absolutely.

We weren't quite done with James, though. His new landlord had given him six months rent-free and a generous build-out allowance for all the modifications. The build-out was just about done when James disappeared. I know this because that landlord called me, too.

"Mr. Tooke, James has gone missing and you're responsible for the rent," the property owner said.

"Come again?" I had no idea what this guy was talking about.

"Well, your business name is on the lease agreement. So you are responsible for the monthly payments." He was professional but forceful.

"I didn't sign anything. What does it say on the lease agreement?"

"Team Tooke. And you're the owner of Team Tooke, so . . ."

Son of a bitch. "Hey, I didn't sign it," I finally told the guy. "He used the business name without my permission. Sorry, but your issue is with James, not me." I felt bad for the guy, who probably lost thousands of dollars as well. He was another victim in James's schemes.

During this whole ordeal, his loyal students were sticking up for him on social media. I was the villain in their eyes. A student who was a police officer, the one I suspected of calling me about the lockout, posted online making veiled threats about kicking my ass if I had to show up at court. Others were dissing Team Tooke as if I ran him out of business and didn't honor our agreement, even though I'd kicked him out of the organization more than a year prior. My name and school were being trashed online, but luckily only a few people were doing it.

But when James ditched town and left them all in the lurch, I think they realized who was telling the truth. A bunch of guys who were talking crap about me wrote me emails about how they had learned the truth and were sorry for what they'd said about me online. The police officer who had called and threatened me wrote me a letter explaining how later James had screwed him out of some money and he'd realized the truth. I held no ill will toward these people and appreciated the apologies. I understood the position they were in. When you truly trust someone, like I have before, you have no reason to believe what they're saying is not true. James fed them these lies, and they had no reason to doubt their veracity.

In the meantime, other students of his began calling me. Some were polite, others were pissed. They wanted Team Tooke to refund them their money but didn't understand that he was using our name without permission. What I did do was give them full credit if they wanted to train at our main location. If they had $250 in unused classes, I credited them $250 to train here. What I couldn't do, unfortunately, was refund students who were too far away to travel to my school.

One good thing that came out of this was a new student who transferred in from the Spring location: Jose Llanas. He started training there in 2008. He had since become an instructor for the Spring location. When Jose started coming to class, it was difficult to read him. He was quiet and aloof. It took a while for him to warm up to his new surroundings, but eventually his passion for jiu-jitsu came out in class. Jose would be instrumental to my school's future. He would go on to become a successful black belt competitor and one of the most technical black belts in the Houston area. Today he is the kids jiu-jitsu head instructor, showing that all dark clouds do indeed have a silver lining and beneath an unassuming, gruff exterior lies a heart of gold—the kids love him!

Over time, Jace made good on his promise and paid me back the full amount. I wish everybody had his character. He's a true and honest friend and a great black belt. James continued to avoid detection, and I learned to forgive him. Life's too short to stay angry at anybody, no matter what they may have done.

I did receive an unexpected test of my forgiveness. A couple of years after that whole mess, I received a letter from a debt collection company. There was an outstanding electric bill for $200. Remember, even the utilities stayed in my name. I shook my head, chuckled a little, and cut a check. At that point it was like a bad joke that I shrugged off.

People have told me I have a good mind for business. Not really, as you have seen. Having a good business mind is partially a matter of not repeating the same stupid things and trying to survive while the stupid things you've done are unfolding. After all that, I think I *finally* learned my lesson: put everything in writing.

More Mentoring

Back before the Spring location issues and SEALFIT, around late summer of 2013, I was sitting in my office (probably working on something I don't enjoy) when the phone rang.

"Mr. Tooke, my name is Bob, and I'm wondering if you'd be interested in a free, twenty-minute evaluation about your school with Stephen Oliver," he said.

My ears perked up. "Yes, that would be great. What's the catch?"

Bob went on with the rest of his spiel, and explained that he represented Stephen Oliver's coaching group and that they'd love to extend me a free phone consultation. I'd known the name Stephen Oliver since I was a young jiu-jitsu student. His name was well established in the martial arts world, and I'm sure I saw his advertisements in *Black Belt* magazine, among others. Master Stephen Oliver has been running schools since he opened his first karate dojo in 1975.

Unfortunately, the call came in about two months before my MMA fight. It's a funny thing about my focus. When we have a tournament coming up, I'm totally focused on preparing myself and my students for the tournament and don't want to be distracted by business stuff. After the tournament, I'm all about working on the business, marketing, tweaking, and making things better. So at this time I was completely focused on teaching my classes and prepping for my MMA fight. I spoke with Stephen a few days later but waited to enroll into his program until after the fight.

It had only been about six months since I'd ended my membership with Lloyd Irvin's coaching group, but I had noted a marked dip in business since then. Things were still pretty good, just not as good as they could have been. Talking to a coach or mentor is a bit like working out. If you keep it up, you continually improve. As you improve, you can make even more advancement in your strength, speed, agility, and overall health. However, if you take a few weeks or a month off, you might still look good, but all of those gains will quickly diminish. My edge was dulling, and I was not as attentive to the business as I know I could have been. My business was getting a little plump. I was ready to head back to the gym.

You see, it wasn't enough for me to know *what* to do. Like a lot of people, I need a coach to keep me accountable so I actually do it. They remind me of the importance behind what I'm doing. Having the knowledge alone is not the same as the drive to put it to work. For me, being in a mastermind group is a way to overcome my tendency to lay back and take it easy. I've said it before: I've got a laziness streak in me.

I knew that Master Oliver could help my business not just because of his own success but because he was also Lloyd Irvin's mentor. Lloyd had learned most of his early business skills from Stephen. Where Lloyd added more value was his extensive success in internet marketing in his online businesses. But in the end, I had originally joined Lloyd because he taught jiu-jitsu and Stephen taught karate. It seems dumb looking back, but at the time I saw them as two different business models. They're not. Stylistically, they are different. But martial arts is about changing lives for the better, and running a service-driven, character-enhancing martial arts school is where Master Oliver is a genius.

By signing up for Stephen Oliver's program, I knew I was in danger of receiving shade from detractors who think he's a karate guy, that is, he runs "belt factories"—quantity over quality. This false notion about karate studios is pervasive within the martial arts community but I think is especially prevalent within the MMA and BJJ community. The thinking is you're either a fighting school that churns out champions slowly, or you're a revolving door making lots of money but creating ineffective martial artists. If you have a lot of students and you're successful, then you must be a sellout. Sadly, there are schools that operate this way, but for a great number of successful academies, nothing could be further from the truth. I think that if you want to focus on champion fighters and keep your school small, that's fantastic! Do what you feel called to do. I love transforming people. I live for the shy, awkward kids who realize they are stronger than they thought and blossom before your eyes. I love imparting strong values like attitude, dedication, respect, family, loyalty, and honor (Ribeiro Jiu-Jitsu style) to students who might otherwise not have good examples. I'm for exposing all of my students to the path of personal growth and development—not just in a physical sense but holistically: mind, body, and spirit.

So you do what you do, and I'll do what I do. In the end, I know those students of mine who compete are some of the toughest martial artists around. Why not have the best of both worlds?

I signed up for Stephen Oliver's course in the early spring of 2014.

Today I continue to rely on his teaching, insight, coaching, and friendship. I once read about how Dr. Atul Gawande, an endocrine surgeon who had reached the highest level of his field, decided to hire a coach—a retired surgeon—to come watch him perform. Why? So he could be an even better surgeon than he already was.

There is no top, only improvement. Never stop improving.

A Place to Call Home

By 2014, we had been in our main location for about four years and had only a year left on our five-year lease. That's when I first toyed with the idea of owning a building. Unlike past locations, this one was spacious and highly visible, and the landlord was great to work with. Still, I thought it might be time to turn rent fees into an investment. Business was doing well, and I had a decent amount of savings in the business account. If I was paying $8,000-plus a month in rent and CAM (common area maintenance) charges, I thought it would be nice if a chunk of that money was going toward building equity.

I called a buddy of mine who was a real estate agent, and he began searching for suitable locations. The first building was only a little ways down the road. It was in a great location but was a little smaller. We met over there, and I could tell it used to be a church. It looked decent from the outside, had good parking and nice visibility from the road, but then I went inside. There were electrical wires hanging everywhere. At first I stayed with the idea. I asked some contractors to give me quotes on the build-out, but they all pretty much said they had no idea how much it would cost. There were too many variables. I couldn't risk a build-out that might be an expensive logistical nightmare, so I passed.

It became apparent that balancing visibility and functionality at an affordable price was going to be the challenge. The best locations with the highest traffic and visibility had astronomically high price tags. The easiest build-outs in okay locations were better priced. The issue was finding one that suited my needs best.

My buddy emailed me a listing one day without a photo. I looked on the map and saw it was less than a mile from our current location. We made an appointment, and I drove over and saw that it was tucked out of sight from the main road behind a plaza with a fitness center. I took the side road to the lot and . . . there was nothing there except weeds and rocks.

The builder met us and showed us the occupied building next door. "This is what I will build you," he said. "Basically, I build you the shell, and then you hire a contractor to complete the inside for you."

That sounded doable. The building was a decent size, with good parking, and close to my location. The visibility was lacking, though. It's nice to have the advertising that comes from people just driving by and noticing that you exist. That wouldn't happen here, not tucked behind another plaza. But only a small percentage of my students came from walk-ins anyway. Most of my enrollments came from all the marketing efforts. Maybe this could work. But before I could decide, I had to do my least favorite thing: crunch the numbers.

After getting various quotes for what it would cost to complete the build-out to my requirements—office space, a private class space, new mats, bathrooms, showers—it looked more and more like this was *the one* (even though the total cost would approach nearly $1 million). I called my buddy, he negotiated the offer, and about a month later I was signing the deposit agreement and construction contract. I was shaking a little—part nervousness, part excitement.

We broke ground soon after, in September 2015, and the construction commenced with excavation of the site, including pouring footings for the foundation, gravel, and all the wonderfully messy, dirty things involved in creating a structure. Except this wonderful dirt was mine!

The construction was projected to be completed by mid-December, and, with my five-year lease set to expire in January 2016, that gave me enough time to complete the interior in about a month, so we could move without any issues.

That was the plan, anyway.

I began visiting the site almost daily as I watched it come together. Except it wasn't coming together as fast as I'd hoped. By Halloween they had poured the footings, spread the gravel, and roughed in the electrical and plumbing conduits through the maze of rebar . . . then things came to a standstill. I didn't have to ask why. It was obvious. With just two months until my lease expired, weather got in the way.

Houston is a pretty wet city anyway, but that season through late autumn and early winter was one of the wettest on record. With it raining heavily almost daily, there was no way they could pour the concrete slab, and that was needed before they could erect the frame. A week delay turned into two weeks and then a month. Thanksgiving came and went. My five-year lease was going to expire on January 31, and I had nowhere to go.

I approached my landlord with trepidation. With an expiring lease and a vacating tenant in a bind, this was a golden opportunity for him to exploit if he wanted to. My fear was soon abated. My landlord was super cool. Instead of making me sign a second five-year lease or even a one-year lease, he gave me an open-ended, month-to-month lease. He could have jacked up the rent, but he didn't; he kept the rest of our agreement exactly the same.

The rains finally let up and construction continued. Oftentimes I'd be there after the crews had left; I'd walk around the steel framework, picturing every final detail in my mind. "This is my office. Over there will be the bathrooms. The trophy display should be right here . . . or maybe over there near the window?" Each day I was getting closer to being in a building of my very own. Not that it was without stress. It took a while to complete the foundation because of rain.

The shell was completed in March 2016. It was time to start constructing the walls, stairs, wiring, plumbing, and all the other necessities. Besides the obvious tasks that required licensed contractors, I had a list of a thousand little tasks that could be performed by just about anybody. I also had a small army of students. The framers began their work in April, and that's when everything came to life. With walls came the reality that this was happening. My students and I had paint parties where it was all hands on deck with buckets of paint and extended paint rollers. By the end of March, I felt optimistic enough to give my landlord the required thirty-day notice: April would be my last month.

Maybe I was overly optimistic.

The construction crews came and left. The wiring was done; the plumbing completed; the drywall hung, taped, and painted. All that was left was the spring floors for the training floor and the tile in the bathrooms. We had a week left. I spent every night that week constructing spring floors. A spring floor consists of a number of three-inch square pieces cut from old mats spaced apart in a grid pattern and glued to the bottom of a thick piece of plywood. That's placed foam-side down on the concrete. But that's not enough. All of these sheets of plywood with the foam are just the base layer, "floating" without any stability. Another layer of plywood is added so that it spans the butt joints of the other sheets and locks them together. Those two layers of plywood must be screwed together. On top of the plywood, we added a layer of plastic to protect from mold, and the actual mats went on top of that.

Our floor was huge. It took over seven thousand screws to complete the plywood sections. Every night, after the last class, I went to the new building and was on my hands and knees with a cordless drill, screwing plywood together. It was excruciating. I began having nightmares about screws and plywood coming apart. My old back injury did not appreciate the added strain no matter how much yoga I'd given it, but it held up. We only needed mats on half the floor to open the doors, so that's what we would do.

We were ready. Almost. The tile in the bathroom still wasn't finished. The tile contractor had told me it would be done two weeks prior to opening, and here we were days away. You can't install a toilet until the floor tile is done. You can't have classes of students and not give them a place to pee. Besides, at least one working bathroom was required for the certificate of occupancy from the city.

In case you didn't know, tile can't be installed in just a few hours. It's a slow process with two stages. First, the thin-set mortar, which locks the tiles to the substrate, needs a day or two to cure. Then, stage two requires two to four days for the grout to set in between the tiles. We were running out of time, and I had to do something.

I called the contractor and laid into him. "I don't need all the bathrooms finished. We don't need the showers done. But I *do need* to have the single-stall, unisex bathroom finished or I can't open!" I thought I'd finally gotten through to him: he made some sort of promise to have them *all* ready for opening day.

He didn't.

But the unisex bathroom was finished! Our first class was held with half the mats, one toilet for dozens of people, and without much fanfare. I was stressing out about it. Then I spoke to Stephen Oliver.

"I love moving into a new location like that," he told me.

"What? Why?" I couldn't understand what was so great about unfinished things.

"Because the students love it. It becomes a part of the lore. Years later they tell new students, 'I remember when we got here. This didn't work, and that was falling apart, but look at it now.'"

Huh. I never considered that. And he was right. The students didn't care that the school wasn't 100 percent done. It was done enough, it was theirs, and it was beautiful.

Eventually every little detail was completed to my satisfaction. Five months later, we held our grand opening. This place was mine.

But on the downside, this place was *mine*. With the mortgage, insurance, utilities, and (drumroll please) taxes, it came out only slightly cheaper than renting. But if one of those big honking air conditioning units fails in the middle of July, I can't just let the landlord deal with it—it's my problem.

It might have taken a little bit more obsession than usual for me to move to our new location, but with a lot of help from friends and student volunteers, and one incredibly slow tiler, we got it done.

I was obsessed with completing a new location in order not to disappoint my students, let people down, or lose money. James's obsession was . . . well, I have no idea, but it sure wasn't responsibility. A healthy obsession can get things done when everything's on the line. It can pull you through the toughest of storms.

Of course, like with the slow tilers, there are some challenges that you have no control over. Winds of change are constantly blowing—sometimes literally. While many storms you face as a business owner you can see coming if you remain vigilant, others are complete surprises. I had a new location and a new mentor, and I had learned a not-so-new lesson (get things in writing). I now needed to learn how to handle the uncontrollable—the weather.

Specifically, Hurricane Harvey.

Compare yourself to who you were yesterday, not to who someone else is today.

—Jordan B. Peterson[20]

CHAPTER 10

Storms and Stupidity

I don't have all the answers. Maybe I should have said that in chapter 1, but then you might not have read this far. I've tried to show you what is possible if you just get started, follow your ambition, interest, or dreams, and then try to figure out the details along the way. You will make mistakes. Some mistakes I've tried to warn you about in advance (getting things in writing, for example), and at the same time, I've hopefully given you permission to try new things and make new mistakes. Because that's the only way we grow; growth comes through trial and error.

Sometimes after teaching a class, I have the students sit on the mat, and we discuss different ideas. Sometimes that lesson is about competing, achieving excellence, or being a good sport, but often the lessons revolve around life outside of the mat: relationships, school, work, health, and mindset. I try to teach my students the lessons that have served me best. At the same time, the lessons I teach remind me of what is true. It's more than just lessons passed on; it's part of my own personal and continued growth. When I search for the right words, lessons, or teachable moments, I'm often reminded of things I've lost sight of.

There's a famous story attributed to the Indian activist Mahatma Gandhi. One day, a worried mother walked for two hours in the sultry Indian heat with her son in tow. She dragged the boy into Gandhi's ashram, hoping he could impart the wisdom to the boy that the mother was unable to.

"Please, my boy will not listen to me," the poor woman begged.

---

20 Jordan B. Peterson, *12 Rules for Life: An Antidote to Chaos* (Toronto: Random House Canada, 2018), 111.

"What is the problem?" Gandhi asked.

"He eats too much sugar. It's bad for him—rots his teeth and gives him stomach issues. Please tell him to stop. He will listen to you."

"Return in two weeks."

The woman thought it strange, but she didn't dare question this great man. She did as she was told and fourteen days later returned with her son.

"I've returned," she said.

"So you have." Gandhi crouched down before the boy, smiled, and said, "You must listen to your mother. Stop eating sugar! You will feel much better."

Appreciative that he did as she had asked but perhaps a little annoyed, the woman nodded and then said, "Thank you, but why did I have to make this long journey twice? Why didn't you tell him the first time?"

"Because two weeks ago," Gandhi explained, "I also ate too much sugar. I first had to give it up myself."

The story is important because it demonstrates what so many people forget: who you are and what you do speaks louder than what you say. So it keeps me honest to impart to my students the lessons I've learned through my experiences. If I made up a fable that everything was easy and fair in jiu-jitsu and in business, and that I never made any mistakes, not only would I be lying, but I'd be doing a disservice to you and my students. After experiencing your first hint of disappointment, failure, or setbacks, you might assume I'm just some lucky guy who has everything figured out. "Too bad I can't be more like Professor Tooke. He's got his shit together." Like I already said, I don't. But my shit is far more organized than it used to be. I'd rather be honest than give you advice about something I know nothing about—and, yes, sometimes I eat a little too much sugar.

Disappointment, Failure, and Gratitude

I've gotten well-acquainted with disappointment and failure. Disappointment is part of life. It's a normal emotion that should be felt and expressed. Pretending things are okay when they're not is called delusion. But by cultivating a growth mindset—that failure is a lesson, not who you are—and then finding something you can invest passion into, like getting obsessed in a healthy way, you then have the power to overcome the largest of disappointments or failures. Feel disappointment, express it, and then realize that it is only temporary. There are far more important things in life that will still be there after you fall. Focus on the bigger things: the people who care about you, the reason you're doing what you're doing (family, love, security, life experience), and all the things you love about life and this world.

Of course, I wasn't always keen on the smaller things when I was younger. Like a lot of kids, I was almost completely self-absorbed and a little greedy. If there was only a little bit of cereal at the bottom of the box, I didn't even think of offering any of it to JP. Finders keepers!

I held on to a portion of this attitude even into my early twenties. I was overly focused on me, my goals, and my problems. But as I matured and learned more about successful people, I understood that this myopia was only holding me back. With my attention on me, I couldn't see how I could help others or even that others could help me. When I began shifting my focus to other people and their issues, concerns, goals, and emotions, a new world opened for me. Over time, I learned to foster an attitude of gratitude.

I encourage you to be grateful for all the riches in your life.

"But Travis," I can hear you saying. "I don't have anything."

That's certainly not true. First, you're reading a book. Even if you got it from a library, stole it, or found it in a dumpster, you have access to printed words. Another thing—you can read! Fourteen percent of people in the world can't read.[21] Even if you can't afford ten seconds of a formal college education, you have access to bookstores, libraries, and a host of online sources to learn the things you need or interest you for almost no cost. You can breathe, see, hear, taste, touch, and smell. Even if some of those senses are missing, you have the others. Maybe you've had awful things happen to you—abuse, neglect, or violence. I can't imagine what you've gone through, and I wouldn't pretend to. But I know that you can still find gratitude only because I've witnessed others who have gone through the worst things imaginable and emerged on the other side victorious and grateful.

Had I not been diagnosed with that freak case of eczema, I might not

---

21 "Literacy Rate, Adult Total (% of People Ages 15 and Above)," The World Bank, 2019, https://data.worldbank.org/indicator/se.adt.litr.zs.

ever have had a positive impact on the hundreds of students whose lives I've touched through martial arts. Had Ingrid not left her hometown to live in Barra, we might never have met.

No matter what you've experienced, no matter what failures, disappointments, abuses, or mistakes have brought you here, you're here. Everything else is a backstory that brought you to this point in time. And whether you realize it or not, you have things in your life that you'd sorely miss if they were gone.

It's so easy to take the mundane and everyday for granted. I catch myself doing it all the time. On cloudy days, I miss sunny days—until a severe drought. I overlook everyday conveniences and luxuries until a major power outage takes most of them away: pumping gas, watching TV, ice for my drinks, or just fresh, home-cooked meals.

I used to struggle with feeling gratitude. I've felt grateful, of course, but cultivating a sense of gratitude and learning to find things to be grateful for used to be difficult for me. Then I learned to think about things I would miss if I no longer had them. Take a moment to think about all the things you have to be grateful for this moment. You have light to read this book by, the eyes to see the words, clean clothes, a brain that can learn new things, an imagination that can picture the scene above, cold running water, and a life in an area with improved sanitation (35 percent of the world's population lack this basic necessity[22]—imagine having uncontained filth and sewage near where you live and work).

You have a lot to be grateful for when you think about it. I know I do. And having gratitude for what I have helps me have the mindset to pursue more. Maybe you don't yet have everything you want. However, there is always someone who would gladly take your place.

If you'd like to experience gratitude firsthand, visit the site of a natural catastrophe. That's what I did. I didn't have to go too far—it was within a mile of my house.

But before I get to that, let's talk about gratefulness that came from a well-played practical joke.

---

22 "Global WASH Fast Facts," Centers for Disease Control and Prevention, April 11, 2016, https://www.cdc.gov/healthywater/global/wash_statistics.html.

A Cheesy T-Shirt Salesman

Sometimes I get deadly serious in this book when it comes to ideas around success, discipline, obsessions, and failure. Despite my soberness at times, I subscribe to a quote attributed to Oscar Wilde: "Life is too important to be taken seriously." I like to have fun . . . often. Sometimes I do goofy things on social media. I once posed with Marko, a student who won gold in the Kid Pan Championship, except I was holding the gold and trophy belt and Marko looked defeated with this caption: "Super proud of Marko for going 12-0 with all submissions and earning all this hardware. But I'm even more proud of myself for going 1-0 against him and taking it all for me!" Other times I just enjoy joking around with my friends. I'm always game for a good time, just as long as nobody gets hurt in the process.

One of the most memorable practical jokes I ever had the honor to play came in December of 2016.

Miguel Castro's Team Tooke Cypress school was growing, and they were having a big celebration for their last day in the old school before moving to the new school. As mentioned, I had trained Miguel from white belt. Since then he's not only mastered BJJ, but he's also grown to be one of my closest friends. The man smiles so much, it's amazing that everyone doesn't consider him their closest friend. Miguel asked me to come to the school to join in the celebration, which I gladly did. But attending wasn't all I had planned for my brown-belted friend.

The students packed into the training area, and we had as much fun as you can have sweating. At the end, Miguel (Professor Miguel to his students) got up and gave an emotional speech. It truly was heartwarming, and Miguel got teary-eyed. This was not unusual for him. While I don't always wear my emotions on my sleeve, Miguel's are almost always pouring out of him. You never wonder what he's feeling. He spoke with gratitude about how much it meant to have his students there and how much he loved them; he thanked me for the opportunity to be a part of Team Tooke. He then started wrapping up class and asked if I had anything to add. Oh boy, did I!

I said a few words—I forget exactly what I said—but then I decided to follow up on this tender, vulnerable moment by hocking some t-shirts. Yes, I made it look like all I wanted was to make a quick buck.

"So, hey!" I said to the class, "We've got some custom t-shirts on sale—

today only!" I then looked at Miguel, who I could tell was a little put off by my sudden sales pitch. My plan was working perfectly. "Miguel, do you have any of the shirts?"

Stunned for a second, as if he didn't want to disrespect me in front of his students, he finally said, "Um . . . I think so. Let me check up front."

"Never mind! I have some right here." I reached into the cardboard box I'd carried in with me and pulled out a black belt. Miguel's black belt.

Oftentimes, black belts are handed out without notice, but it's usually awarded on promotion day—when everyone gets together in one big event to see who's getting what belt. Brown belts who have been brown belts for a while are always suspicious they'll earn theirs on that day. I didn't want Miguel to have the luxury of suspicion.

I've mentioned before about the value a black belt represents. It requires years of hard work, discipline, persistence, and mat time. It's always a thrill to hand out a new belt. While many people have it on their bucket lists, few do what it takes to actually achieve it. Awarding Miguel's black belt was an extra special privilege for me. Not only was Miguel my dear friend, but his was also the first black belt I awarded to someone who started with me as a white belt.

When I removed the belt from the box instead of a cheesy t-shirt, Miguel's face showed a weird mixture of relief, surprise, and honor. Like I said, you never have to guess what he's feeling. I tied it on him, and then we hugged. It was water works all over again. I could have awarded it at my school during promotions day, but I wanted him to share this honor with his students who had been with him for years. It's my best and most memorable practical joke to date, one that I will cherish until my dying day.

Those weren't the only water works that would be memorable. It turned out that Mother Nature had planned some water works of her own only months later.

Bad Moon Rising

August of 2017 was a busy month for me. I still compete a few times a year, but that August was especially busy. Earlier in the month, I traveled up to Seattle for the International Brazilian Jiu-Jitsu Federation Open Tournament to represent Ribeiro Jiu-Jitsu, the team of my sensei

instructor Saulo Ribeiro. We had a blast! The team finished third overall, and I managed to win first place in the Master 2, Middleweight
Division. Of course, tournaments are always more fun when you get to
take home gold.

Then I went back home for two weeks to prepare for the big tournament: the World Master Jiu-Jitsu IBJJF Championship held in Las Vegas
at the end of each August. It's a huge event with an international field of
BJJ martial artists competing in an amazing arena at the Las Vegas Con-
vention Center. The atmosphere can reach the fever pitch of a professional sporting event as competitors sweat it out in front of grandstands
full of spectators. It's super fun and awesome on so many levels. Even
if you don't study jiu-jitsu, the trip is worth it to watch these amazing
competitors.

The dates for that year's competition were August 24–26. But first
I was going to spend a few days in San Diego training with Saulo Ribeiro and others on his team at his University of Jiu-Jitsu. It was going
to be an exciting week, and I was flying out August 18. Like most people,
I started watching the weather before I left. I was mainly concerned with
San Diego and Las Vegas. They are typically hot and dry that time of
year, but I wanted to make sure. The meteorologist mentioned a little
tropical storm in the Caribbean named Harvey, which Texans needed
to pay attention to, but on the day I left, the forecasted path showed it
curving in to the Gulf of Mexico and probably making landfall somewhere between the Guadalajara Peninsula and Corpus Christi. So Houston wouldn't be affected!

I had a blast in San Diego and got in some world-class training before a bunch of us headed to Las Vegas to meet up with some of my
students for the championship. In the meantime, I had a chance to call
Ingrid. She told me Harvey was turning toward Texas a little more, but
it still shouldn't be a big deal. Ingrid is the sensible, pragmatic one in the
relationship, so this was a valid concern. I'm more of a "let's see what
happens" kind of guy. Houston is about sixty miles inland from Galves-
ton, which is usually enough land to take a lot of punch out of cyclonic
storms. The maximum winds sustained at the coastline dissipate quickly the farther a storm travels. I wasn't worried, and I continued on to
Las Vegas without a care.

What I didn't consider was rain.

The world championships arrived with much excitement, and the Ribeiro team had another stellar event. It was three days of one great match after another. However, I kept hearing about Harvey. The storm had quickly ramped up to a whopping category-four storm on the Saffir-Simpson scale, with maximum sustained winds at over 130 miles per hour. I still wasn't too concerned. Those winds occur only around the eye. The storm is huge, and that storm center is relatively tiny. I still thought the winds were all I needed to worry about.

The championships ended and the team prepared for the trip home. Though I didn't fare so well this time, Team Ribeiro placed in both the male and female categories. The male team finished third, and the female team finished second! My student Melissa Lozano won two individual silver medals in her matches. I was super proud of my team as I always am. We left the venue and enjoyed the highly anticipated Mayweather vs. McGregor boxing match.

The highs and lows of the tournament faded the next day as we entered the airport and began making calls home. Harvey was bearing down on Houston. The storm had lost strength as I predicted. But what no one had predicted is that it had stopped moving. Harvey had made himself comfortable and slowed to a crawl over the Greater Houston area. Things did not look good.

Melissa and I decided to divert our flight to Dallas, though there were still a few flights to Houston available. Meanwhile some of my students stayed optimistic. Their flights hadn't been cancelled, and they saw no reason they would be. Harvey was pretty much a gusty rainstorm by this point, right?

We were taxiing onto the tarmac when I received a text from one of my students. It read something like, "Ha ha, professor, we've boarded our flight. You should've stayed positive."

Minutes later, Houston's airport, George Bush Intercontinental, closed to all incoming flights. My students' flight was cancelled, and they had to deplane. "Told ya so!" I texted.

Melissa and I rented a car in Dallas and drove into the storm. We were rerouted multiple times due to flooded underpasses and roads, and the rain was just pelting our windshield, making it difficult to see. We finally made it to our homes and waited out the rest of the storm. Houston was a disaster area. The previous spring—2016, when my new location had opened—was one of the wettest on record, the proverbial five-hun-dred-year flood that insurance companies and forecasters talk about all the time. But Harvey was far worse. It inched through Houston at a mind-numbing pace of two miles per hour, all faucets open on full blast.

Fortunately my school and house stayed safe, as did the homes of most of my friends and family. Others were not so fortunate.

When Harvey finally moved on a couple of days later, the totals were in. Almost thirty inches of rain had fallen on our area within three days. For comparison, the "five-hundred-year flood" from the previous year's spring was around twenty inches. A five-hundred-year flood is supposed to be an event that has a one in five hundred chance of happening any given year, and Houston suffered two such events in sequential years. I don't know what they odds of that are, but it's not a lottery I was happy to have won.

Aftermath

Although what remained of Harvey's eye was now well north, the worst wasn't over. Creeks and rivers were still being fed by the runoff from fields, parking lots, and roads, and they continued to rise. At its peak, Cy-press Creek, which usually averages fifteen feet across, was over a half-mile wide. The creek is about three miles from my house, but in the days following Harvey, it was too close for my comfort.

Houston looked like a surreal warzone. Cars were almost completely submerged—at least the ones I could still see. Roadways and highways had become river channels with the tops of their streetlights sticking out. Everywhere around the downtown area, people were traveling by boat. Downtown Houston had turned into Water World.

A good friend of mine, Mark Malfa, who runs an alligator gar fishing guide service, ran his airboat for two straight days, rescuing dozens of people and pets who were stranded in flooded homes. They had no idea if the floods would engulf their homes completely as had happened in New Orleans with Katrina, so they were happy to have a ride to safety.

Inspired, I told my brother that we should take my fishing boat out and see who we could help.

"Are you crazy?" JP said.

"What do you mean?" I replied, a bit perplexed.

"Do you remember what happened last time we took it out fishing?"

"Um . . . yeah."

"How the motor stalled and we had trouble getting it restarted? That's fine in the middle of calm lake. What happens when it stalls with a bunch of people in it, and we're being dragged under a flooded overpass?"

He made a valid point. I didn't want to rescue people only to deliver them to their deaths. We helped out in other ways instead. JP drove his truck around, and we waded through water checking on people and even saved one elderly dog from his flooded kennel for his concerned owners.

The bigger story was how the city came together. Nobody cared about skin color, who you voted for in 2016, or whether you were rich or poor. If someone needed help, someone else was there answering the call. It was wonderful to see people coming together for the greater good.

We opened the school the day after the power was restored. Many students were not working because of the flooding, and we wanted to give them a place where they could come and forget about the disaster for a little bit. We just announced through the social networks that we were open and they could come by and train if they wanted. And they came. For both me and them, opening the school provided a welcome sense of structure in a world full of chaos.

Some students had relatively minor flooding—some floors and walls had to be replaced. Others virtually lost their homes. We decided to come together and host a few benefits for the students affected. We hosted one such event at my academy, and Robby Rabadi held one in Austin. Everyone gave, and though it wasn't a lot of money, the recipients were thankful for the gesture.

Only a few weeks later, Houston was well on its way down the long path to recovery. Businesses were reopened; construction crews were flooding in—pardon the pun—from all over the country to help.

The meteorologists had forecasted Harvey's path accurately about four days before landfall. They failed to predict the storm to stall.

I predicted a quick recovery from the flooding. I didn't expect my business to stall.

Breaking Even—Again

While only a small percentage of my students were badly affected by the storm, my new enrollments plummeted after Harvey. The Cypress Creek flood cut right through the center of my marketing focus. With any martial arts school, there's an expected and predictable turnover rate, even when you make great efforts to minimize it. People move on for various reasons. They literally move out of the area, get a job on the other side of town, lose interest, or change their mind about training. The latter is something we, as coaches, can work to control but there will always be some level of attrition. All the coaching, marketing, and management in the world isn't going to bring the rate of attrition down to zero. It's an accepted part of the business. What surprised me is that the revolving door began moving in only one direction—out.

Half the population I relied on for new enrollments now had bigger things to worry about. On August 20, 2017, they might have seen my ad and thought, "I think I'd like to try a free class." Four days later and they have no house, car, or maybe not even a job. Not the ideal time for someone to commit to martial arts training. As a result, my total enrollments were dwindling. I still had my core group of diehards who were there no matter what, plus a number of up-and-coming students who were loyal and consistent. This kept the classes looking deceptively full. What was missing were the new white belts. As the damage from Harvey continued after the storm, the number of cancellations was soon surpassing the number of new students.

What's worse is that this realization didn't sink in for me right away.

Though I had been a student of Stephen Oliver's for a few years by this point, I had not focused on the "numbers" as well as I should have, once again. What do I mean by "numbers"? The number of free introductory students, the number of students who enroll after their introductory class, total new enrollments for the month, and similar items. I wasn't oblivious to the numbers, but when things get tight, an entrepreneur must know these numbers fully and accurately. My brother JP is our manager, and during this time he relayed to me how things were slower than usual. Regardless, I allowed this to go on without taking enough action. It was no one's responsibility but mine—it's my business, and even if I hired somebody to track the items, I would still do what I need to manage and grow the business. I wish I could blame Harvey for the downturn. If I point at the storm, though, I'd have four fingers pointing back at me.

Here's the tricky thing about watching the numbers: if you're not watching the trends, too, the numbers only tell half the story. I had been watching the numbers like this: "Oh, enrollments are up 3 percent this month, that's pretty cool." But the next month they'd be down 3 percent. Not cool. The month after that, up 2 percent. Then down 3 percent. Up 4 percent. Down 5 percent. Do you see the picture? I didn't pay enough attention to this. By the end of the year, I was down 20 percent and wondering what the hell happened.

I wish I could say that it started the month after Harvey—September brought a big enough dip that caused me to take a look at the bigger picture. It was worse than I had thought. I'd been on a barely noticeable but steady trend downward, only made critical by the flooding.

I had advanced as a businessman, but I still wasn't a black belt.

The most frustrating thing about sales and marketing in a martial arts business—heck, pretty much any business, when I think about it—is you're never 100 percent sure what's working and what isn't. You can try one campaign that falls flat; meanwhile, you're running fifteen to twenty other things, like Facebook or Instagram ads, YouTube commercials, newspaper inserts, free demonstration events, postcards, whatever. Things you think might be bad sometimes work great. Others? Not so much. And no matter how well you track sources, you're not always sure where the new students heard about you. They say it takes a person seeing an ad seven times before it registers in their brain. For some, that might mean seeing a billboard, radio ad, TV spot, etc.—and then the last thing they see is a Google ad on a website, so that's what they tell you when they finally enroll. Had it not been for all the other campaigns, though, they still might not have "heard" about you. You just don't know for certain.

At this point, with all the drama in Houston and then seeing my numbers tumble, I got a little cynical. I'd been grinding at my passion all these years. I felt like Sisyphus pushing the boulder uphill—one slip, and it's back to the beginning. I'd been driving, pushing, and working only to see another step backward. For a brief period, I lost my drive and was just going through the motions.

I'd watched family members go into major depressive episodes before—

how stuck they would get. Each time, I'd want to shake them and say, "Snap out of it." I knew that it wouldn't work and that would be the worst thing I could do; however, it didn't stop the desire.

Well, over a period of weeks, I slid into a funk. I wouldn't label it a full-on depression. But as much as I *know* that disappointment is part of life and that I should always push forward, I had hit a boundary and didn't want to push anymore. My finances were suffering because of the downturn, and I cut my personal salary to almost nothing so I could stay afloat. Ingrid and I were having some tough times in our relationship (due in large part to my newly found pessimism), and my long-held desires and goals seemed to have vanished.

I wasn't in a full-blown panic about the dip in business, but for the first time since the beginning of the school, I didn't see the business bounce back. Mostly I was in denial this entire period. I kept thinking, *This will be the month. Things will improve.* But things didn't get better. It was like I was expecting things to improve by just doing the same old things that we had always done.

In 2018, for a short time, I realized that I was not doing well emotionally. I'd gotten complacent and lost my edge—my drive, my aggressiveness, was gone.

It might have been really dark. Had I let this cynical thinking drag me down, I imagine I could've lost everything I'd worked for. It was that scary. Hardly anybody knew—I only told my brother and a few friends that I was struggling. They did the right things—they listened and empathized. Some had been through depression, and I was like, "Holy shit, this is what you were feeling?" Except I know it was worse for them. It opened my eyes to just how inescapable this heavy malaise of depression can be. Before, I tried to have compassion for people with depression. Now, I see that this is a sinister, pervasive disease that insidiously creeps into your life and sticks to your mindset like phlegm in your lungs after a bad head cold.

But something small inside of me kept me going. Maybe it was the years of positive conditioning, my sense of responsibility to those in my care, or just good old-fashioned stubbornness. Something, though, kept getting me out of bed (though I wanted to huddle in the blankets and forget that the world existed for a while), going to work out, and showing up at school to greet the students, joke around with the coaches, and listen to others' struggles. Maybe it was my *why*, the passion I brought to this, my lifelong dream. I don't know for sure. All I know is I kept going through the motions, with only a few around me knowing what was really going on.

That's so important, by the way. Having that support team of friends, family, or mentors you can tell anything to. I didn't want to tell them. It was so difficult to open up. But I still did.

What turned it around for me, I think, was a coaching call with Stephen Oliver in late 2018. I explained what was going on over the past year, that the business was suffering, and that I even considered leaving the group out of a sense of shame for not reflecting the amazing coaching I was receiving. Like every good coach should, he listened, validated that what I was going through was real and serious, and then helped me devise a plan. I had something to shoot for again, a direction to head in, and that was what I needed.

At the end of 2018, things started turning around. Yes, I was struggling at that time when I'm certain many thought I had my proverbial shit together. I probably still don't, and that's fine with me. Life is a process of continual challenge and growth. Every year we experience four seasons: spring, summer, autumn, and winter. Even in Brazil, the weather patterns change. Those outside seasons are symbolic of the seasons in your life and in mine. I had an autumn—a fall, you might say—and had survived a dark winter. The year 2018 was a rebirth—a time for new growth. It was spring again. Subsequently, 2019 was the best year for our business since we opened. I plan to keep it this way, but I'm ready for the challenges that lie ahead. In hindsight, I'm thankful for the challenge and opportunity of having to overcome a difficult situation. It taught me to be prepared for the figurative storms of change in business. Most importantly, it taught me how to climb out from the valley and get back on top.

This seasonal pattern is especially true for leaders. Being a leader has highs and lows. The highs include watching teammates or students have that *aha!* moment, or when you challenge them and they accomplish something they never thought they could. With those highs come the lows of feeling like an impostor, or being so strong in one area but failing at another and letting that make you feel like you're a complete failure.

As certain as I am that the sun will rise tomorrow, I know the future holds even more highs and lows. I've learned from the valleys and mountains I've already traversed and am better prepared for the unknown. Don't let yourself get stuck in any valley, no matter how dark it seems at the bottom. There are hills to climb, mountains to conquer. Join me and then laugh at how small that place looks once you rise above it.

The future is unexplored—it's an exciting adventure.

It is not I who create myself, rather I happen to myself.
—Carl Jung[23]

*I have tried to live my life such that in the hour of
my death I would feel joy rather than fear.*
—Witold Pilecki[24]

*Whether or not you can never become great at
something, you can always become better at it. Don't
ever forget that! And don't say, "I'll never be good."
You can become better! And one day you'll wake up
and you'll find out how good you actually became.*
—attributed to Neil deGrasse Tyson

CHAPTER 11

Giving and Gratitude

In the spring of this year, 2019, my team and I celebrated fourteen years of Team Tooke. An anniversary is just another day. It's the same with holidays like New Year's Day or birthdays. Yet it serves as a guidepost to look back at how far you've come and how far you have to go. You can reflect on any day—you can set a resolution on a Wednesday in the middle of March if you want. But for some reason, we get deep on these special occasions.

It was during one of these moments about four years ago when I first toyed with the idea of writing a book. Yes, even that idea was fraught with fear and negative thinking. Just because I've been through a lot doesn't mean I'm a perfect fount of wisdom. I wondered, *Who am I to write a book? Why would I waste my time on something nobody would care about or*

---

23 Carl Jung, *The Collected Works of C.G. Jung, Volume 11: Psychology and Religion: West and East,* edited and translated by Gerhard Adler and F. C. Hull (New York: Bollingen, 1958), 259.
24 Quoted in Mark Manson, *Everything Is F*cked,* 10.

read? I know you recognize that voice and have heard it whisper to you, too. For a time I believed it. I went about my business, learning, growing, failing, and trying again.

Except the idea didn't go away.

Remember the power of *what if* thinking? Instead of thinking about how nobody would read this, I thought, *What if someone does read this, and it helps them in a positive way? What if that person then helps a few others?* Suddenly, with the idea that I only have to help a few, the book seemed worth the trouble.

In late 2016, I finally took action. Because of that decision, you're reading these words today. My intention wasn't to share my story at first. I just wanted to share some of the life lessons I've learned through my years training jiu-jitsu. But I learned that it's my story—what I went through and what I learned—that matters. I'm nothing special. Many, many people could have gone through what I've gone through and have probably succeeded and learned their lessons more quickly. My hope is to convince you that you don't have to let fear, circumstances, or failure stop you from pursuing what you want in life. With that in mind, here are my parting lessons.

Challenge Yourself

A lot of people hear "martial arts" and picture little kids running around in white gis learning how to punch, block, maybe break a board, and face bullies. To some extent this is true. I'm proud of our adult students, but a good portion of my students are under eighteen. Our coaches and I take the role of teacher seriously. While we love having fun with the kids, we also want to challenge them, push them, and stretch them to do more than they think they're capable of. The kids are great. Their parents, on the other hand . . .

Don't get me wrong: most parents are super. In fact, all successful martial arts schools owe a great deal of their success to supportive families. Parents love their kids and want them to learn self-defense, gain confidence, and try things they're interested in, whether that's BJJ, piano, violin, or sports. It's great to expose kids to a variety of activities in the hopes they'll find something they're passionate about. But when parents are doing these things for selfish motives, there's an issue.

Parents are meant to guide kids. But all too often, I witness overbearing parents. They want their kid to excel and be the best. By itself, the desire to achieve excellence isn't a bad thing, but not when a parent is seeking self-gratification from their kids' accomplishments. Oftentimes, they end up pushing the kid away from the very thing they love. It's unhealthy, toxic, and the kids soon stop enjoying the activity. This can lead to burnout and even quitting.

The flipside to that mistake is just as bad. Sometimes a kid is taught a new technique that they're having difficulty mastering. Other kids seem to learn it more quickly, and this discourages them. They've been taught the fixed mindset and believe "I'm not good at this." Or they see other kids who can do thirty push-ups while they struggle with three. Comparison is a legitimate human trait—we all do it. This is a learning opportunity where the coaches and I can teach them to focus on their own progress and try beating their previous best. Still, during these moments a lot of kids (and adults) want to quit. Some parents are great and say, "No. Get through this. You started and you're going to finish your commitment."

I wish this were true in all situations.

Instead, a number of parents let their kids quit because things are getting "too hard" or it's "too difficult for him" or "they don't like it anymore." Maybe they want their kids to like them, or maybe in a misguided way they're trying to protect their kids from ever feeling discouraged. But they're doing their kids a great disservice. Facing and overcoming challenges is what allows us to achieve anything in life. If a child is taught to quit—or the parent models quitting—as soon as things get tough, what's that going to do to her for the rest of her life?

She had trouble learning the cash register. Quit. The guy in the other department was rude. Quit. Going to the gym three times a week turned out to be harder than sitting on the sofa binging Netflix. Quit. Where does she end up in life? Unless she finds a way to challenge herself emotionally and physically and learn she can push through it, she's doomed to a disappointing life.

There's a balance. The best parents are those who are encouraging, yet firm—loving and tough when needed. These are the parents who don't care if other parents are judging them: their child's needs come first. They offer a shoulder, a hug, and then a pat on the backside as they push them to try again and again and again. These parents are modeling a growth mindset, the idea that, "No, you're not good at this yet. But with practice and hard work, let's see how far you can go!"

But maybe you're not a parent or a kid. You're an adult who does adult things and enjoys adulting every day. What does all of this have to do with you? Maybe you had an upbringing like mine. Alcoholism, arguing, divorce, and even violence. There's a lot of debate around whether spanking is necessary. I received worse.

Though we get along great and work together at the school every day now, when my father was younger, he had anger issues, and discipline done in anger benefits no one. His own upbringing was far worse than mine, and he lacked the self-control to parent without anger. If I ticked him off, sometimes he'd lash out with the crack of the belt or an open hand; I remember as a ten-year-old helping him on a construction job, and he whacked me on the leg with a four-foot level—all that force transmitted to my skin through two narrow rails. I can still recall the stinging feeling to this day. Another time he slapped my face so hard he had to keep me home from school—that's how bad the welt was. He always felt terrible after these altercations. This time he apologized profusely and covered the handprint with foundation before I went to school.

In part due to this "discipline," I struggled with a sense of inferiority for years. And maybe your upbringing was far worse. I know I had it pretty easy compared to some of you.

But as with my Navy rejection, the past only brought you to where you are today. Now you have to be your own parent. No, you *get* to be your own parent. This means not letting yourself off the hook when things get tough. It also means giving yourself a shoulder to cry on and telling yourself that it's okay to mess up. Beating yourself up doesn't lead to mastery; it leads to misery. Be the parent to you that you might not have had growing up. And then challenge yourself.

Earn Your Belt

Discipline is a funny word. For me it conjures images of military-type people who are up at four a.m., do a hundred push-ups, drink only water, and put in a twelve-hour workday, accomplishing more in a week than most people do in a year. The word discipline also makes some people like me think of a parent's leather belt.

To me, discipline means pushing yourself to do things that might be painful, uncomfortable, or difficult until those actions become a habit. Being consistent with your actions, making small steps daily. The Jocko Willinks and Richard Bransons of the world didn't obtain their level of discipline in a moment. Neither were they born saying, "Let's do this!" Like most skills, discipline is learnable.

I've said it before: I have a tendency to be lazy. Of course, I wouldn't be where I am without a level of discipline—getting up and doing what I need to do when I don't feel like it. I love this quote sometimes attributed to hothead basketball coach Bobby Knight: "Do what has to be done, when it has to be done, as well as it can be done, and do it that way every time." These are good words to live by. Some people get overly focused on one area of life—career for instance—and assume that Bobby Knight's wisdom only applies there. It applies to every area of life: when you are playing with your kids, teaching a class, relaxing with your partner—do it and do it as well as you can. Whatever you're doing in the present moment, it's important to you and deserves your full attention; otherwise you'd be doing something else. Whatever you do, give it your full love and attention.

In the end, discipline is like a muscle that can be developed. Those of us in martial arts value our belts because the discipline and discomfort of training is immense. There's nothing more physically exhausting and challenging at an emotional level than when someone taps you out (makes you submit) over and over again. It's the challenge that causes you to grow, try harder, and reexamine your approach. And when you get that belt, all of that sweat, frustration, and exhaustion has meaning. You wear that belt with pride and look forward to the next challenge.

That's why I challenge my students. That's why you need to challenge yourself—physically, if you can, because a physical challenge is the easiest to identify and keep score of. It can be as simple as committing to competing in your first local tournament or as complex as winning the IBJJF World Championship. Regardless of where you are healthwise, create a challenge today. Scale your challenge appropriately for where you are at, but whatever target you choose, stay committed.

After a poor health report from his doctor, motivational speaker Zig Ziglar decided to start running. In his mid-forties and overweight, he made his first challenge easy: run to the neighbor's mailbox. He almost didn't make it. The next challenge was to run one block. Then a block plus one mailbox. And he did it. Every. Single. Day. Each time, he aimed to run just a bit farther. But it wasn't always easy. After a number of weeks of keeping his commitment, he had to fly out to a speaking engagement in Seattle (he lived in Dallas). He flew back later that same evening. By the time he got home, it was four a.m. His alarm for running was set at 5:30 a.m., meaning he'd only get ninety minutes of sleep. He seriously thought about skipping a day, but he knew if he skipped even one day, the next time skipping would be easier. He set the alarm, went to bed, and woke up feeling miserable, wanting to throw that clock out the window. The run was awful; the day was unproductive. But he writes this in *Over the Top*: "Having said that [I had a bad day], I suppose my next statement will surprise you. I consider that one of the most important choices I've ever made. I kept my commitment, and keeping my commitment that time made it easier to do it the next time, the next, and the next."[25]

We all face obstacles as we challenge ourselves to grow. They can be external ones like travel delays, weather (hurricanes), economic changes; or internal obstacles like fear, apathy, a feeling of failure, or depression. But when you have a commitment, find your *why*, and grow your passion, you overcome these obstacles one by one. When you accomplish your challenge at the end, you see all the ways in which you've grown.

My students usually start jiu-jitsu for one of two reasons: they either want to learn the cool moves and be able defend themselves, or they want to get in shape. But as they progress, the list of ways they've grown is so much longer than just "getting in shape" or "learning cool moves." This is true with anything that challenges you: learning a business skill, practicing an art, getting a degree, or becoming an awesome parent—you start off with one thing you are trying to get good at, and then the self-discovery you gain in the process molds you into a new person. I started learning jiu-jitsu because I thought it was cool-looking. My commitment to it has molded me into who I am today and taught me almost everything that I hold to be true and valuable. But it took a

---

25 Zig Ziglar, *Over the Top* (Nashville: Thomas Nelson, 1994).

long time. It took a lot of failure, a lot of pain, a lot of defeat, and some failed friendships. These are not all good things, but good came out of them. The bad experiences build resilience so you're stronger next time. In my experience, no bad thing has ever come from challenging yourself to grow.

Find True Success

I love social media. It allows me to reach out to the martial arts community, find events I want to go to, celebrate wins, rally support for people in need, and have fun joking around with friends and associates. If you're in business, you're almost forced to have a presence on social media these days. But as much as I enjoy using it, there's a dark side to the Instagrams and Facebooks of the world.

It's not real.

Think about when you first meet somebody. Everything you discuss is superficial. Small talk varies from the weather to fishing or sports—you're looking for ways to connect and are presenting your best self. We all want to be liked. Sometimes you hit it off and the relationship gets deeper. Maybe at this point you discuss your opinions, values, sex, politics. Then the relationship becomes a deep friendship. Trust is formed. You feel the freedom to get vulnerable and be yourself. The conversations can then go from football scores to secrets you have never shared with anyone.

You never reach that level of connection and authenticity on social media.

Ever.

Almost the entire relationship is at that top, superficial level of weather, sports, and jokes, or one-sided political views and everyone always trying to be their best selves—or fake selves.

Most of my Facebook friends are not my real friends—even the ones who in real life actually *are* my real friends. Your Facebook friends are not your *real* friends either. These days, you can't even be sure that what they look like on social media is how they really look, what with filters that make people look young, thin, and wrinkle-free. On social media people tend to be upbeat all the time and have a "perfect" life. *Here we are by the pool. This is our family vacation. Look at my new car!* These are great, but when I'm with my real friends, I can tell them what areas I'm struggling in and the challenges I'm going through. I can listen to them say they're worried about their business—things you probably won't see on social media. YouTube, Facebook, Instagram, and Twitter may one day all go away and be replaced by new technologies. The people who love you online today could hate you tomorrow.

True success is found in real relationships. Your family and a few special friends are where you're going to find a deeper purpose to life. And if you don't have a family you can trust, then adopt a circle of people with whom you can connect deeply—but only a handful that really love you and that you love as well. And value real human connection. I can't be every student's and coach's best friend, but I can take time to connect emotionally with everyone I meet. That feels *so* real and stays with you longer than any feeling you get from social media.

My success is rooted in my life with Ingrid. She has exposed me to things I never would have considered. When I used to visit new cities for tournaments, the tournament would be pretty much the only thing on my agenda. But now Ingrid comes with me, and she loves travel, photography, and everything French. Left on my own, I would be far less interested in the history and food and architectural sites than I am now. Ingrid has cultured me. I never would have thought it, but when we travel to the European IBJJF Championship, we now make sure we take extra time to explore other European countries. I even know how to sniff and swirl a glass of wine and comment on how it pairs with some cheese. My younger self would have laughed at me, but now I actually enjoy it.

Ingrid, in turn, took up jiu-jitsu herself and made it to blue belt. After that, she stepped away from the mat, but I'm trying to coax her back. That's the effect relationships and people you love can have on your life— you learn to appreciate what they are passionate about.

True success is also learning to just be. Being able to experience the full range of emotion and not look for an immediate escape. No matter what happens to your goals, dreams, and plans and regardless of what setbacks you might face, learn to experience the joy and gratitude for this moment. This is probably the most difficult thing to master. But when you learn to appreciate and hold gratitude for something as small as lunch with a friend, then you have a higher level of control over your mental health—you are free to embrace all of life's moments fully.

I can almost hear you say, "But Travis, what about all that stuff about taking risks, leaning into fear, and growing?" That is all true. I think happiness only comes through making progress toward things that you believe matter. But we get to determine what progress looks like. A writer can have a goal for a thousand words a day. But on one busy day she only writes a sentence. Did she fail? No. She still made progress. Have a preference for an outcome, but have no judgment for the outcome that occurs.

It's like winning. If I defeat an opponent in a match, does that mean I'm a better fighter than I was yesterday? Maybe, maybe not. Defeating someone is not necessarily the same as winning. Winning means being better than I was before—it means I've made progress. Just because I beat someone else doesn't mean that I am better than who I was yesterday. And if I lose, that doesn't mean that I am worse than I was yesterday. When determining progress, always measure against yourself. Never compare yourself to others, especially to those people on the internet.

This is what your purpose is made of. As we discussed in chapter 5, you get to choose your purpose. When you are pursuing your purpose, it doesn't matter if you "succeed" in one moment and "fail" in another. Friends, family, progress, and gratitude. Cultivate these, and you will never feel like a failure again.

Challenge Your Beliefs

Earlier I discussed the benefits of challenging yourself—giving yourself a goal and committing to it. There's a specific reason for this: you will never be able to go back to who you were before. Once you annihilate a concept you held about who you are and what you're capable of—when you do something you never thought you could—the door of possibilities opens up. What other things can you achieve that you thought you couldn't?

For me, SEALFIT did that. I thought it would just be a fun, physically demanding challenge. What I didn't expect was that, through the leverage of teamwork, I carried loads and endured pain I never would have done on my own. I expanded my self-imposed limits beyond what I believed I could.

But what are beliefs, really? They are nothing more than stories. We all love a good story. It's how we relate as human beings. Jesus and the Buddha's teachings survive today because they were told in parables—pearls of wisdom shared through a simple narrative. Even if you've never set foot in church, you probably still know the story of the Good Samaritan.

Beliefs are the stories—parables—we tell ourselves so our brains can make sense of our world and how we fit into it.

But what if all of these stories are false? We can discover our stories by asking questions.

Go skydiving.

"Oh, Travis, I could never do that," you could say.

Really? What if some deranged psychopath kidnapped your family and held them at gunpoint until you went skydiving? You'd be asking how much time you have to book the plane.

But you said you could "never" do that. Was that true? Or was it only true under certain circumstances?

I hear it all the time. "I love jiu-jitsu, professor, but I couldn't compete in a tournament."

"I can't do fifty push-ups."

"I couldn't teach a class."

"I can't learn Portuguese." (This one was mine.)

These are just stories we tell ourselves. They can be about getting healthy, quitting drinking, learning to dance, starting a business, earning a black belt, or writing a book. We have stories we've told ourselves so long they begin to sound like the truth.

The above examples might seem like obvious limiting beliefs, but there are insidious beliefs so well disguised that nobody questions them. Here's one I've heard: "We only study Gracie Jiu-Jitsu because it's the purest." In other words, all other styles of jiu-jitsu are bastard creations because they deviate from the one, true Brazilian Jiu-Jitsu: Gracie Jiu-jitsu. To many people, this seems legitimate (it also seems a little like religious fanaticism).

I'm familiar with the Gracie family. Beside Royce Gracie, there are many other members of the family who train and fight in jiu-jitsu. They are all successful fighters in their own right and have paved the way for the golden age of jiu-jitsu that we all enjoy today. But here's the thing: not one of them fights the same as the other. They've all developed their own variations and styles. While their contributions to the art are beyond measure, to believe there's a "pure" Gracie style is inaccurate.

So how do we counter these false beliefs—stories—we have about ourselves? On a larger scale, how do we determine if the widely accepted statements we hear are really just "fake news"?

Be willing to question everything. Challenge it. Don't let anything go into your ears without the willingness to determine if that's the truth. If your doctor says, "The best way for you to lose weight is to diet and exercise," question it! There was a time when nearly every doctor was advocating for low- or no-fat diets. Modern evidence suggests that is not necessarily a good thing. Smoking was also considered a healthy activity just a few decades ago.

Question—but don't become a closed-minded skeptic who believes nothing. I love when a student questions why we perform a certain move. But she needs to go practice that technique and learn it well, and then, when she's learned it well, she can go find out if there's a better way. At some point, you need to stop questioning and trust. The wisdom is in knowing when.

Most importantly, question every concept you have about yourself. Every thought, passing idea, or assumed truth must be examined and cross-examined.

"I wish I could run a marathon," you might catch yourself saying as you see Suzie's progress on Facebook.

"Wait, why couldn't I?" you ask.

"Because I don't have the time," your mind answers.

"Is that really true? Do I have to watch all twenty episodes of *Rick and Morty* this weekend, or could I start a running program instead?" (*Rick and Morty* is the best!)

"But I'll be too tired."

"Maybe. Or maybe I'll build up energy and feel good about myself."

"But I'm so fat. People will make fun of me huffing and puffing."

"Maybe they will. Do I really care what those people think?"

"What will I feel when I succeed?" Oh, now there's a question to ask.

How about, "I wish I could be a black belt one day, but I'm already forty-five years old."

Guess what? Ten years is going to pass by anyway. Do you want to be a fifty-five-year-old still wishing for the same things, or do you want to be a fifty-five-year-old black belt?

This internal conversation could go on. Every response deserves to be questioned. Questioning a statement casts doubt on it, and nothing changes a belief quicker than doubt.

Seriously, though, take the time to step back from the stories you tell yourself and explore whether they are true. Question every piece of information that is handed to you as a fact: that meme with the quote (hint: Einstein didn't say that thing about a fish climbing a tree); the political pundit you usually agree with; the advice your landscaper gives you on fertilizer; and even your doctor's diagnosis. I don't mean that you should distrust everything, but a little healthy skepticism, especially about the things you blindly accept about yourself and your so-called limitations, goes a long way.

Be a Leader

As I look back at what I've experienced and learned and look forward to the promise of the future, I realize leadership is part of life. And we are all leaders to some degree. If you help anybody learn a new skill, raise a child, or do anything worthwhile, there will be people looking to you for leadership. But if you hope to open a business, start a school, or advance in martial arts, your leadership role may be more clearly defined.

Leadership has inherent highs and lows. One day you could witness a student experience an *aha!* moment or watch as they do something that they never believed they could do before. When I see this, it reminds me of when I had those moments as a student. Those are some of the greatest, most life-changing experiences a human being can have. Those are the moments when my beliefs changed and I realized I could do something I previously thought was impossible—like the first time that I, as a brown belt, defeated a black belt in competition in Brazil.

But I can have a moment like that and the next day have this feeling of impostor syndrome. Like when I watched my business flounder in late 2017 and 2018. When you're a leader, while you may be strong in one role (teaching, in my case), you still have to perform in a lot of other roles as well. And when I forget it's normal that I'm not equally strong in every single area, it can lead to feelings of inadequacy.

When I catch these feelings of inadequacy, this belief I'm supposed to be Super Travis and awesome at everything, I stop and remind myself that I'm good just the way I am and getting better every day. That's how I would talk to a student feeling the same way. No martial artist, no fighter, no person excels at everything. Leadership is not about perfection; it's about being honest and vulnerable about your imperfection. When I do that, I give others permission to be imperfect, too. There are no perfect people, and would anyone like them anyway?

Above all, a big part of leadership is giving. Most importantly, it's giving the best you have to give to both yourself and to others. As leaders, there will be times when we give our all and receive back little or nothing. It's not always give-and-take. The challenge is to continue to give and trust that there will always be a return, one that will be greater than what you gave. This might seem woo-woo. It's not. I think it's just part of human nature. If you don't give, almost nobody will give to you. If you give and take, you'll break even. But if you give consistently, enough givers will come into your life to make up for the takers. For more on this philosophy, check out the book *Give and Take* by Adam M. Grant.[26]

However, be smart in your giving. I'm not suggesting you give away your clothes, car, and home expecting the universe to give it all back plus some. There are some real bad guys who love taking advantage of those people. There's a balance. When you give intelligently, though, you will never give away more than you receive, because it always comes back in greater quantities.

Lastly, leadership requires having a vision for the future. It's easy for us to get mired in the grind of everyday work, but once in a while we need to put those activities on hold so we can work on ourselves, and bring future goals to the present moment. We call this working *on* the business instead of *in* the business. When you have a clear, compelling vision for where you want to go, you're willing to take risks, commit to your goal, and are willing to be open minded enough to question your beliefs, there's no force on earth that can stop you.

---

26 Adam Grant, *Give and Take: A Revolutionary Approach to Success* (New York: Viking, 2013).

Final Thoughts

Every moment is precious. The older I get the more I appreciate this truth. It's so easy to get hung up on our past or lost in the daydreams of our future that we forget about right now. This moment is a small slice of our lives, a step along each of our journeys. If you spend all your time in the past and future, you never learn to enjoy the present, which is all you really have anyway.

There's an expression that says the black belt is the last belt you will ever wear. To make the most of your journey, you must enjoy and cherish every belt along the way. Many students are so concerned with "the next belt" that they miss some of the most precious and life-changing moments of their current belt. It's a trap to become so fixated on the end, the tangible reward, that you forget the priceless value of the experience itself.

So don't waste time on idle activities that don't bring you joy. Pursue those things that flame your interest, passion, and dreams. Stick to your gut instinct and do what you believe in and love, even in the face of haters. In time, they will go away, as will any short-term drama. What will be left will be the result of the decisions you and your team/family/ business partners made over the years. Do the thing that you feel is right, even when you're afraid, and be willing to alter your course when you veer to far from your target. You will find success by growing and not giving into fear.

I've covered a lot about my life in this book. But I'm just a kid from the trailer park who fell in love with jiu-jitsu. What I really want you to learn are the lessons I learned—some harder than others. If I were to wrap up the lessons into one paragraph that you could refer to, it would go like this:

Pursue the things that interest you. When something catches your attention, follow it to see where it takes you—it may become your purpose in this world. Pursue that purpose with all you have, develop a healthy obsession that motivates and inspires you. Along the way, learn to be resourceful. Resourcefulness trumps actual resources any day because the former is as unlimited as your imagination. Build relationships, whether it's already-strong family relations or a new family of friends who become like brothers and sisters. When difficult times arise (and you can bet they will), you will need to lean on these core relationships for support; be there for them to lean on, too. When life and people try to knock you down, get up. Get physical. An unhealthy body destroys a capable mind. Develop resiliency—a willingness to adapt, respond, and grow in the face of challenges. As you pursue your healthy obsession, have faith in the process to get you there. Your attempts to reach goals might fall short, but the process will buoy you and keep you going. Continue your efforts long enough and your results will likely surpass your original goals. And in the end, practice gratitude. Be grateful for the lessons learned from setbacks, the pain of defeat, and the thrill of victory. Learn to be grateful for anything in your life you would miss if it were gone tomorrow. Love yourself, love others, and if you're like me, love jiu-jitsu.

And with that thought, I want to express gratitude to you, the reader. Thank you for your time, energy, and willingness to share in my journey. My deepest hope is that what I've given you through these pages will help you become a slightly better version of who you were yesterday.

Afterword

Starting Over Again

My story was told—this book was finished and ready to go to publication—then the strangest thing happened: I got to experience the beginning all over again. I was so inspired by the experience that I had to ask the publisher to squeeze in just one more story. It's a story that involves long travel, exotic animals, poverty, and some of the happiest people on earth . . . and, of course, jiu-jitsu.

I first met Voddie Baucham in 2012 when he was pastoring a local church. He entered my school like most of my students: eager and optimistic. He smiled easily, and everyone liked him. His charisma, commanding presence, and authenticity has made him a highly sought-after speaker and successful author. Best of all, Voddie fell in love with jiu-jitsu just as I had. Though already in his forties, he didn't let age interfere with the mindset that he could learn and master new things. He had the goal of losing weight and getting back to the fitness level he enjoyed as a collegiate football player. Jiu-jitsu was now a part of that goal.

A few years of solid progress later, Voddie, by then a blue belt, felt called to the mission field in Zambia. If you don't know where Zambia is, it's a country in south-central Africa just a little larger than Texas. As much as he was excited about this next chapter, he admitted that he'd miss jiu-jitsu because it didn't exist in Zambia. We said our goodbyes and promised to keep in touch. Over the next several years, we kept up through phone and email, and he'd drop into the school to train whenever his speaking engagements brought him back to the Houston area.

Well, in early 2019, he called me with exciting news. "I'm starting a jiu-jitsu school!"

"What?" I was excited for him but a little confused. He always had a compelling way of adapting biblical parables for modern life. Was this school some sort of parable?

"I've been training with a friend, and others want to learn."

During his newfound life in Zambia, he had met a chiropractor (what is it with jiu-jitsu and chiropractors?) who was also a former jiu-jitsu student longing for his days on the mat. They began training together, which piqued the interest of others in the community. Soon, they had the first Brazilian Jiu-Jitsu school in Zambia.

"I'd love for you to come out here and give some classes to the team. What do you think?"

Well, I love traveling the world, and I'd never been to Africa before. It didn't take me long to say yes. We planned the trip for November, right before Thanksgiving. And after a long series of flights that took me from Houston to Chicago to Ethiopia, before finally arriving in the Zambian capital of Lusaka—almost a full day, twenty-three hours, in a plane—I arrived at an airport whose entire building was equal to about half a terminal at Houston's George Bush Intercontinental Airport. Voddie met me there with a welcoming smile, hugged me, and took me to dinner before dropping me at the quaint home of my host, a man named Tim Byrd who worked with their church and was a new Brazilian Jiu-Jitsu (BJJ) junkie to boot.

The next day I got to experience Zambia in the full daylight. A little foggy from jetlag, I wasn't too sleepy to marvel at the greenery. Everything was so lush and beautiful. "You're lucky," Tim told me. "It's been dry and brown around here, but in the past few days we got enough rain to bring everything to life."

I had come at the perfect time—the monsoon season hadn't yet started and the sun was out. It was sticky and warm because, though it was late autumn back home, it was late spring south of the equator. The city of Lusaka is actually as or less advanced than I thought. It is still very much in the "developing" stages of a developing country. Other areas resembled the Barra in Rio, with one major difference: despite the poverty, the crime rate is pretty low. And although the city doesn't have the architectural spectacle of a big American city—most of the buildings are under three stories high—the people, most of whom speak English, seem content with their lives.

The next day, I taught my first class in Africa. The school, Lusaka BJJ Club, was in a small room off a large metal-walled warehouse-like structure. The main facility is a CrossFit center, which I was surprised to see there, but the school itself was smaller than my dad's garage. However, the cramped space didn't affect anyone's attitude. The students were so happy to train with a black belt!

I spent all day—the first of five—in this cramped space with Voddie, his partner Pierce, and their students. We had all the basics a jiu-jit-su school needs: sweat dripping, students training, and endless smiles. These students had never been exposed to training like this, and they were 100 percent focused and committed to making the most of the week. No discredit to my American students, who are awesome; it's just that these people had such humble lives, and yet they poured their hearts into mastering these techniques. I might not fully understand their customs, beliefs, or culture as a whole, but we were connected in those moments on the mat—people with a shared purpose.

For those few days in Lusaka, I got to reexperience the joy of my garage days. Teaching for the pure love of the art. I took at least as much enjoyment in teaching them as they did in learning.

In my spare hours, I experienced as much as I could—I mean, c'mon, I was in freaking Africa! I remember walking around thinking, "Wow, I'm actually here!" I had always thought maybe I'd get to visit that far-away continent "someday," but now I was here. The day before returning home, Voddie took me on safari in the Chaminuka game reserve. Because of the fresh rains, *all* the animals were out in the savannah: warthogs, zebras, and giraffes. I even walked a cheetah on a leash! It was incredible seeing these beautiful animals in their homeland instead of a zoo. It was a real dream come true.

I also learned that as bad as Houston drivers can be, driving here is much better than driving in Lusaka. Because of the poverty, most people walk. The city streets resembled photographs I'd seen of refugees fleeing a war-torn area, though these people were just walking to and from work. Forget driving at night. Voddie had a friend of his act as my driver, and when he drove me through the mostly unlit streets, you wouldn't see the pedestrians walking in the road until you were twenty feet from them. I don't know how many people we narrowly missed—I kept thinking that we were surely going to hit someone. Besides that, there are laws against hauling freight or giving rides to people in the backs of trucks, so to avoid detection, these dark nighttime roads were also packed with trucks full of freight and people. Riding in that car at night was the only time I felt any danger there.

In the end, Africa was an experience I wouldn't trade for anything. I love teaching and enjoy every chance I get to be an ambassador for the art that's become my life. Any opportunity to share the lessons I've learned is both an honor and a privilege. The passion and love given by the students of Lusaka BJJ Club reminded me of my own—it reunited me with my past self.

Despite the success I've enjoyed with the help of my team, I've never forgotten my roots. I'm still *Travis*—just a kid from the trailer park. I still learn new things every day, still laugh out loud at wildly inappropriate jokes, and still feel a sense of pride each time I enter the school. I love jiu-jitsu. I have ambitious goals that are inspired by my desire to positively impact people's lives. But in a sense, the trip to Zambia brought me full circle. It was a visceral reminder of my beginnings, and it filled me with gratitude.

As you embark on your journey, or travel further down the road you're already on, remember your *why*. For me the trip underscored that my journey is not only about reaching personal and financial goals or success and winning. It's a journey of love that I'd continue to follow even without the rest. May your path be inspired by the same love.

Acknowledgments

To my cousin, Andrew Craig: thanks for always treating me as a brother and for taking me with you on your journey to the top of the mixed martial arts world. We've created memories I would never trade . . . and I'm still the only undefeated MMA fighter in the family. ;-)

To Master Stephen Oliver: thank you for showing me the path of great business success while cultivating the highest degree of integrity and student service. My/Our leadership is a reflection of your leadership.

To Sensei Saulo and Alexandre "Xande" Ribeiro: thank you for showing me the purest form of jiu-jitsu I have ever experienced. Flow. Pressure. Finish!

To my team of instructors (in no particular order): Professor Todd Moore, Professor Jose Llanas, Professor Cameron Graves, and Coach Anthony Martinez. The success of our academy is the result of your continued dedication to serve our students to the highest standard.

To my parents: thank you for supporting and believing in me. We have survived challenging and even dark times together. Now we can smile and laugh together. I love you both.

To my loving and beautiful wife: *Oi meu amor* . . . Thank you for taking a leap of faith into the unknown and moving across the equator to be with me. You inspire me to be a better man, and I look forward to growing old with you. *Um beijo, Docinho!*

To my brother John "JP" Tooke, my right-hand man, my best friend: you fill my life with laughter and joy even though you've had to put up with having me as a big brother for so many years. You're an amazing person, and I love you.

To all the Team Tooke students: this book, our team, and most of my life's work only exist because of you. I'm honored to do what I love for a living and am eternally grateful that you have given me the opportunity to serve you all. Thank you.

Travis Tooke has been the master instructor and CEO of Team Tooke Mixed Martial Arts for the past fifteen years. He earned his black belt in Brazilian Jiu-Jitsu from Carlos Gracie Jr. and currently holds the rank of fourth-degree black belt. Travis has been teaching jiu-jitsu for over twenty years and has trained thousands of students, including UFC veterans Andrew Craig and Yves Edwards. He is also an active jiu-jitsu competitor.

Travis lives in Houston with his wife Ingrid, and, besides teaching and training in jiu-jitsu, he is a student of life. He loves expanding his knowledge, growing his business, traveling the world, fishing, and learning to play guitar.

www.ingramcontent.com/pod-product-compliance
Lightning Source LLC
Chambersburg PA
CBHW051423090426
42737CB00014B/2801